MW00982414

Journal Entries of a
Trepid Sailor

Jacquelyn Watt

Journal Entries of a
Trepid Sailor

JACQUELYN WATT

ANNOTATION
PRESS
A DIVISION OF WINEPRESS PUBLISHING GROUP

© 2008 by Jacquelyn Watt. All rights reserved.

Annotation Press (a division of WinePress Publishing, PO Box 428, Enumclaw, WA 98022) functions only as book publisher. As such, the ultimate design, content, editorial accuracy, and views expressed or implied in this work are those of the author.

No part of this publication may be reproduced, stored in a retrieval system, or transmitted in any way by any means—electronic, mechanical, photocopy, recording, or otherwise—without the prior permission of the copyright holder, except as provided by USA copyright law.

Unless otherwise noted, all Scriptures are taken from the *New American Standard Bible,* © 1960, 1963, 1968, 1971, 1972, 1973, 1975, 1977 by The Lockman Foundation. Used by permission.

ISBN 13: 978-1-59977-018-5
ISBN 10: 1-59977-018-0
Library of Congress Catalog Card Number: 2007910287

Contents

Acknowledgments

SUPPORT

"Captain" Bob Watt—husband of 40 years
Joan Conover—twin of 60 years

REPAIRS & MAINTENANCE

Dr. Patricia Gorai, Dr. Clarice Sackett
and Group Health Cooperative

TECHNICAL

Hal Perry of NIC Technologies
Tim Shook
Jordan Kellogg, Verizon Wireless

INSPIRATION

Tor, Anabelle, Alex, and Max
Grandchildren Extraordinaire

SPECIAL MENTION

Sailing Vessel—Shadowfax
Dingy-Shadow

MECHANICAL ASSISTANCE

Dan and Raeann Taylor
Action Marine Services

ENCOURAGEMENT

All my many email friends:
Josephsons, Lofgrens, Beatties, Conovers, the Watt clan, my SPS "family," Bassett & Wyse group, Weymouths, Hansons, Harts Holmans, Arndts, Zitkoviches, and others who urged me to continue on with my journal entries during our voyage as a way of vicariously living the experience along with us. A special thanks to Nancy and Linda for their powerful prayers.

PHOTOGRAPHY

Courtesy of Captain Bob

CARVING

Captain Bob's artwork resulting from a lifetime love of wood

Introduction

This book is a foray into the world of Pacific Northwest sailing by a former bookkeeper. The use of journal entries to describe the many adventures while sailing up the Inside Passage from Seattle to Alaska kept the author connected to her accounting roots and formed a basis for a literary organization of events. This is a journal of a sailor new to the sailing experience, but knowledgeable enough to respect (and fear) the tides, currents, weather, waves, and whirlpools of the area. Not intrepid, but a trepid sailor.

This journey also was an opportunity to study the land, islands, and some of the waterways the Pacific Northwest Indians plied for centuries until supplanted by later settlers.

We spent our time well. Captain Bob brought his carving tools and fashioned a paddle, leaving many woodchips and the smell of yellow cedar on board the Shadowfax. I busied myself by investigating the history of the various anchorages and circuitous routes of the Inside Passage that the Shadowfax traveled using a computer, the internet, and books. We were well entertained on our voyage.

Because Captain Bob's carving inspiration was based on art forms of the Pacific Northwest Indians, it only seemed appropriate to include pictures of some of his carved depictions of Ravens, Cadborosauruses, Thunderbirds, and others whose spirits surely still haunt the waterways of the Inside Passage.

The information in this book is meant to be as reliable as imagination, gossip, the internet, and research books can make it.

Journal Entry #01
Twin Passages
2006

The year 2006 marks the end of twin passages by twin sisters on the East and West Coast of the United States. One sister spent a year on the 51-foot Morgan S-V (sailing vessel) Growltiger, sailing from Virginia to Europe and the Mediterranean, then back across the Atlantic to the Caribbean and home again—a trip of approximately 10,000 miles and 19 countries, ending in June 2006. The other twin sailed on the 40-foot S-V Shadowfax up the Inside Passage from Seattle, Washington to Thomas Bay—north of Petersburg Alaska, starting in May and ending in August of 2006—a three month and 2,000 mile journey.

The eastern twin was an experienced sailor, the western twin a veritable novice to sailing with only a year of actual sailing experience. Where the eastern twin fearlessly braved ocean swells and hurricanes, the western twin was more comfortable within sight of land.

Strong currents, whirlpools, rapids and large tidal swings of the Inside Passage were challenges that the Growltiger didn't have to deal with on its travels. Growltiger only had to deal with trade winds, Hurricane Delta in the Canary Islands, and pirates off the coast of Morocco. No biting Alaskan horseflies or snarling seals for the Growltiger!

The eastern twin sailed forth with a laptop computer, navigation software, radar, a VHF radio, SSB radio, a ham license, a satellite phone, sail-mail (email services for boats via marine high fidelity single sideband radio), an EPIRB (rescue beacon), and an emergency life raft. The western twin sailed forth with radar, Garmin GPS software, a VHF radio, a laptop computer with a broadband air-card, a three watt phone booster, a four foot cell phone antenna, and a foldable port-a-boat. The sailors achieved their objective of successful navigation and communication with the outer world despite using very different modes to do so.

Both twins sailed out of their respective harbors and both returned unscathed with wonderful memories and a feeling of successful completion of a lifelong goal.

This is the story of the western twin's voyage.*

---

*The eastern twin's tale is documented by Gregory Conover on the website: www.sv-growltiger.com

Journal Entry #02
Mink Poop on the Batteries
March 28, 2006
Bellevue, Washington

In the process of readying our sailboat, Shadowfax, for the upcoming boating season we have been contemplating the option of adding either a wind or solar power generation source to our equipment. The idea of "free" power from either the wind or sun is a tempting idea in this day and age of huge fuel costs and seekers can find a wealth of products available from catalogs, local stores, and internet sources.

One particular product intrigued us—a portable wind generator. "Portable" means it can easily be put up as needed in the wind by using a halyard in the cockpit area to hoist the generator and its spinning blades aloft. In addition, when mounted on the rear rail of the boat and the generator (which is in the water), it becomes a tow behind "torpedo" busily generating power as you sail or motor. The torpedo—with an appropriate assortment of kelp, fronds, and drift—could also function as a sea anchor, making it a multi-tasking piece of equipment. It almost seems magical!

My sister and her husband introduced us to this electrical wonder when we visited them on their sailing voyage from Virginia to Europe and back. (We visited them during a two-week Caribbean part of their trip so as to avoid hurricanes and pirates.) They purchased this unit before they left on their cruise and never used it in the eight months they had been on the water. They proudly showed us the unused unit in its original box which was stored under the navigation station onboard. The complexity of the dual setup evidentially prevented the installation and use of the charger. (I was intrigued enough to visit the manufacturer's website after we returned home and have been kicking myself ever since because we didn't tinker with the generator in the water. I know wind generators work in the wind, but in the water too?)

The other power option is a solar panel and this is one innovation that we are knowledgeable and comfortable with. We have used solar panels successfully for lighting and for water pumping at our cabin in the San Juan Islands for 14 years. Our system is simple—using only four golf cart batteries, two 55 watt Kyocera solar panels, a charge controller, and huge copper wire (2/0) running the 100+ feet from the solar panels to the house. We have never inverted the power in the house, preferring to use 12 volt fixtures and wiring for simplicity. Our cabin is a little like a spacious boat, electrically speaking.

Unlike a boat, however, only two electrical repairs have been necessary since the installation of the system. One was the maintenance and eventual replacement due to old age of the golf cart batteries. The other was the total failure of our electrical system, not exactly an "act of God." I guess one would have to call it an "act of mink." Arriving one evening, we were astonished when our power would not switch on, so I stooped low enough to see underneath the cabin where the batteries were stored. I realized rather quickly that the batteries and I had company. A family of mink had moved in and the stench was eye-watering!

The mink pantry and garbage dump were located inside the shredded insulation that used to cover the underside of our cabin's floor and the latrine was set up on top of the uncovered batteries. Mounds of reeking mink poop interlaced with rotting and partially digested crab shells had shorted out our batteries. As I crouched in the dark, scraping the battery terminals, sitting in a pile of mink excrement, eyes watering from the pungent odor, I told myself that it couldn't get any worse than this. Just then the flashlight I held between my knees reflected two bright pinpoints of light shining back at me a few feet from where I sat. Part of the odor under the house was due to a dead and decaying mink whose open eyes were staring at me as I scraped terminals in the dark.

We will have the normal run-of-the-mill battery maintenance and repair on the Shadowfax, and we will be prepared when the time comes to replace the batteries whether we are using wind, engine, or solar power for charging. If we add the water-towed torpedo to the options with this new wind/water charger, we may have a new series of challenges. (For example, I can envision a leviathan attempting to eat the torpedo as a snack). At least we will never have to scrape mink poop off the ship's batteries. They will be sealed.

Journal Entry #03
Alaska Here We Come
May 10, 2006
Meydenbauer Bay, Bellevue, Washington

We had an auspicious start to our sailing voyage from Seattle to Alaska—sunny weather, a nice breeze, and a bald eagle diving and soaring within 20 feet of our vessel as we started into the Montlake Ship Canal. The eagle was in the process of trying to catch baby ducklings that were scrambling madly over the water with their mother. The combination of a defensive mother duck and the startling effect of our vessel motoring near the ducklings prevented the babies from becoming an eagle snack—at least for the time being.

The Montlake Bridge was the first of five bridges we had to open to reach Puget Sound from Lake Washington—each requiring the use of appropriate loud blasts from our horn and the subsequent answering blasts from the bridge tenders. Since it was just past 9:00 A.M., I am sure we irritated some of the commuters trying to make it to work on time. It gives one quite a feeling of power to be able to legally bring traffic to a halt—all four lanes of it in some cases. We traveled through the Montlake "Cut," into Lake Union, and along the ship canal through Ballard to the Locks, where we would ride the water down to Puget Sound in a marine "elevator" operated by the Army Corp of Engineers. All this occurred without mishap and our trip through the small locks went smoothly. We had one final railroad bridge to open and then we were free to head north with a 15-18 knot westerly wind blowing. This is great sailing!

Our first stop was Hat Island off of Everett where we spent a peaceful night in the marina and our crew toured the island. After a 5:45 A.M. start from Hat Island, an exhilarating sail up Saratoga Passage, a trip through Deception Pass and its strong currents, we raced along with a southwesterly wind and arrived at Stuart Island at 8:00 P.M. We traveled approximately 90 miles. We hit speeds of seven to eight knots frequently and even pulled off a 10 knot reading surfing down a wave.

We spent our second night at Stuart Island putting us ahead of our non-schedule. We are allowing the weather and tides to dictate our plans. We just know we have four months to get to our destination (hopefully Alaska) and back.

Before we left Bellevue, we managed to entice a couple with wonderful credentials to make up the rest of our crew. Dan is a mechanic who operates a marine boat repair shop and his wife, Raeann, assists him. She is also a black belt in karate. Both of them are EMT's and brought a first aid kit with them. Additionally they are volunteer firefighters, so we are covered medically, mechanically, physically, and pyrotechnically.

After Stuart Island, we cleared Canadian customs at Bedwell Harbor, put up the Canadian Flag, and headed for Ganges Harbor on Saltspring Island. The town of Ganges is a great place to shop and sightsee.

We spent the next morning looking over the town and checking out the Saturday Market filled with rustic crafts, produce, and baked goods. Now for Nanaimo and the crossing of Georgia Straits! So far we have only used 8.5 gallons of diesel. Sailing is certainly the way to go in these days of high fuel prices!

The Shadowfax actually feels alive while sailing and motoring, unlike when it was moored at dock in Meydenbauer Bay. It smells different too—the freshly ground coffee and the spices packed on board for seasonings have fragranced the cabin.

I purchased real nutmeg and mace spices while in the Caribbean and brought them, and a grater, along with us. The only problem I had was figuring out that the nutmeg was inside the nut shell and it wasn't easy to grate the shell. I eventually gave up after becoming discouraged and I put the plastic bag of nutmeg nuts, the grater, and mace in the small console in our salon table. Every time someone opens the console to get out the teapot we get a wonderful whiff of spices, so it worked out well.

We ate dinner in the cockpit while enjoying the view of Nanaimo and Protection Island in the late evening sun. We had halibut with candied ginger, a tossed salad, rice, buttered asparagus, and homemade rye bread from the Ganges Saturday Market. We washed it all down with a glass of chardonnay wine.

The only casualty of the day was yet another of my special pans. Shadowfax seems to have a problem with my cooking pans, and not the cheap variety either. Last year my prized pressure cooker was destroyed; this year and this meal it was my large Aircor pan. Somehow, while the halibut was sautéing in the succulent ginger juice, a pressure seal was formed as the pan sat (as per the directions), forming a vacuum and the pan lid ended up being horribly deformed with a permanent large indent.

As for internet access with my Verizon aircard, laptop computer, PowerMax antenna booster, and four foot cell phone antenna, I have had no problems anywhere I have tried it so far. I did notice that coverage at Ganges was better this year than last—probably because of the additional booster equipment. The real test comes further north.

Journal Entry #04
Ghosts of Owners Past
May 15, 2006
Gulf Islands, BC

My husband's family has a long maritime history, including an alleged relative known as Captain Kidd, the Pirate. Even my side of the family has Norwegian seafarers in the background with last names such as Anderson and Jacobson. So we definitely have a connection to the sea on both sides of our genealogy.

The family seems to accumulate boats. The Lark is a 27-foot wooden boat built in the Grandy Shipyards of Seattle in the late 1950's. It was purchased almost new by Robert Watt Sr. and cruised for many years in the Pacific Northwest under his captaincy. After his death, we inherited the boat and used it for 18 years until we purchased the Shadowfax. But we had no intentions of getting rid of the Lark. No way! Now our daughter owns title to the Lark and she and her family continue to cruise the Northwest waters.

I have always been fascinated by what I call the "ghosts" left on a vessel by past owners. The inventory left on a boat tells a story about both the departed owners and the boat's history. With the Lark we had the opportunity to know the previous owner, so we knew that when we ran across miscellaneous parts, bolts, screws, or wires, they had a reason for being there, so we never removed them. This came in handy a number of times, and I always felt as if my father-in-law was still around subtly helping us when something needed to be fixed.

The Shadowfax has a different feel to it, perhaps because the previous owners were not deceased and chose instead to sell the vessel. Abandonment through sale versus death seems to make the difference. The Shadowfax has had to fend for itself through various owners and as a result seems to be more self-sufficient than the Lark. Each previous owner has unknowingly left a tantalizing whiff of history behind. The first aid kit has differing vessel names, including Quest and Water-Baby. The outstanding box of spare bolts, screws, and sailing hardware left by one of the prior owners gives evidence of provision against disaster—knowledge only acquired through the experience of not having a needed part.

We had planned to change the name of Shadowfax when we purchased the boat, but the graphics on the side of the boat were so large that the expense of replacing the lettering combined with the fact that the name wasn't that bad made us decide to keep the name. The sailboat is named for Gandolph's horse in *Lord of the Rings,* and the rocking motion during sail does seem like a gentle canter. I wonder if the Shadowfax knows that its transitory ownership days are over and will settle down to permanency, perhaps even having a benign helpful "ghost" like the Lark has someday.

Journal Entry #05
Desolation Sound!
May 17, 2006

After leaving Nanaimo, we got up at 6:00 A.M. and headed across the Straits of Georgia for Texada Island and Malaspina Straits. Again, we had sunshine with great northwesterly winds and as a result, made excellent time. We made our crossing on one tack and in two hours. This sailing tack lasted from Nanaimo to Pender Harbor which is very lazy sailing for the Pacific Northwest area. Our progress was facilitated by the fact that an area known as "Whiskey Gulf" was not active. Whiskey Gulf is an area well publicized on Channel 16—the Coast Guard calling and emergency radio channel. Active means that the Canadian Coast Guard is engaged in torpedo practice. Trespassers create a flurry of conversation on Channel 16 with warnings to stay clear of the area unless they want to become an accidental target. Apparently this activity often occurs during the height of the boating season in the summer, so it was interesting that Whiskey Gulf was inactive when we crossed in the early "off" season. Maybe the Coast Guard needed more targets than the early season provided.

With the good sailing winds and sunshine we decided to push on to the end of Texada Island and a snug harbor called Stuart Bay where we spent the night. It was another tough dinner in the cockpit; this time curry with rice, coconut, dried fruit, nuts, tossed salad and finished off with homemade apple cobbler. An eagle and three ravens provided entertainment on the nearby shore. The eagle was attempting to eat his dinner on the rocks and the ravens spent quite a bit of time attempting to steal his meal. The ravens even plucked at tender eagle tail feathers which resulted in loud indignant squawks from the victim and countering jeers from the attackers.

From Stuart Bay we pushed on with light winds to Lund Harbor for a bit of sightseeing and shopping and then on to Priedeux Haven for the night. We were able to raise our Tri-radial Drifter (Spinnaker) in the light wind for the first time on the voyage. And we couldn't resist dropping a buzz-bomb (a type of fishing lure) in the water off Sara Point in hopes of catching something, but we had no luck. Guess the fish knew we were cooking a beautiful roast of beef from the Thrifty Foods in Nanaimo and weren't willing to sacrifice themselves for the "surf" portion of "Surf n' Turf."

As we neared the entrance to Priedeux Haven, we joined a sailboat "parade" entering the harbor. The boats quietly slipped through the water without wakes—which made for quite a different sight than in the height of the summer boating season when huge power boats form the parade and the harbor is jam-packed with vessels at anchor. The harbor is protected from prevailing winds and currents so the air and water get relatively warm, even in the middle of May. We measured 83 degrees in the cockpit and

68 degrees in the water, so we donned swimsuits and gingerly went swimming. Our crew whined a little about the water temperature until we all realized what a photo opportunity it was for swimmers to be showcased by the snowy peaks surrounding the harbor. Shivering arms and legs forgotten, we all cavorted and swam back and forth like seals in the cold water in an attempt to pose for the perfect picture.

Journal Entry #06
Solo at Teakerne
May 18, 2006
Teakerne, Dent Rapids and Shoal Bay

We managed a first for us…anchoring as the sole sailboat in front of the waterfall at Teakerne Arm. The waterfall plunges about 150 vertical feet from Lake Cassel above—a white cascade captured at the end of a crevice-shaped mini-bay. The spray misted us in the evening as we ate dinner in the cockpit. The temperature was about 80 degrees and it was a sunny day without any clouds or wind—weather more like August than May.

The guys hiked up to the lake and went swimming after an aborted attempt to shower in the waterfall. The footing was too treacherous with all the oyster shells, mussels, and seaweed to get under the falls without serious mishap, so they opted for the quarter of a mile climb to the lake above.

The only near disaster occurred when the sun shower exploded above the hatch over the navigation station. First we heard the sound of running water. Then water spewed down the hatch, nearly dousing the laptop computer. I couldn't move faster if I had a blow torch at my feet.

After dark, the moon and stars were bright in the sky above the Teakerne Cliffs, and the Big Dipper was pointing at the North Star—or maybe it was our anchor light, which was bright enough to illuminate the cliffs surrounding the Shadowfax in our anchorage, wedged snugly as we were between them. In the morning, loon calls became our alarm clock and we woke to another sunny, warm day. We cast a few half-hearted buzz bombs off the front bow before breakfast with no luck.

Then we were off to attempt the three sets of rapids on our way to Shoal Bay. Raeann was pretty calm about the rapids until I handed her some reading matter. (Am I mean, or what?) After flipping through it, she approached us in the cockpit, book in hand, saying, "Are you sure we want to do this? They talk about boats with 50 horsepower engines having trouble, and starting at least an hour before slack to make it through."

We assured her we had gone through many times before, not mentioning that most of those times were with a 260 Horsepower 27-foot power boat, not a 40-foot sailboat with a 40-horsepower engine. The sailboat has one horsepower per foot and the power boat has ten horsepower, so we knew we were in for a challenge.

We negotiated all the rapids with no problem and headed for Shoal Bay expecting to find an empty dock. Instead we found two large Grand Banks trawlers and one huge 80-foot yacht that was heading for the dock with 13 more Grand Bank trawlers in hot pursuit of dock space. Needless to say, the dock is not that large, and we were fended off by the yachters and the owners of Shoal Bay.

The power boaters were extremely relieved that we were willing to anchor the Shadowfax instead of rafting up with their boating club. (We didn't feel we had a much of a choice.) The group was celebrating the fiftieth anniversary of Grand Banks Trawlers by heading for Wrangell, Alaska. We hoped they reached it long before we do.

A good plan would be to check with their commodore to obtain their travel itinerary so we can prevent future conflicts. They are a great bunch of people, but they are intimidating in such large numbers, so we would prefer to limit our contact to as few occasions as possible.

We had a clear night in our anchorage and we had a great view from our cockpit looking out over the snowy mountains of Phillips Arm. We saw the Big Dipper again and I noticed it was still pointing at our anchor light.

Tomorrow we will be attacking Greene Point Rapids, Whirlpool Rapids, and then, hopefully, a quiet moorage at Forward Harbor.

Journal Entry #07
Lagoon Cove
May 20 & 21, 2006
Lagoon Cove and Echo Bay

With northwest winds of approximately 12-18 knots, we were able to tack most of the way up Johnstone Straits from Forward Harbor to make Lagoon Cove by the 5:00 P.M. daily "Happy Hour." Bill Barber hosted an excellent gathering (as usual) of about 10 people, which is pretty good for this early in the season. Bill provided prawns and the Shadowfax provided a Mardi Gras King Cake, complete with a small gold baby strategically placed in Bill's piece of cake to make sure he would be hosting the next social event, which seemed appropriate.

The next day's forecast was for a nasty low front with gale southeasterly winds to attack the area, so we decided to forego exploring at Village Island's abandoned Indian Settlement and head for Echo Bay's snug harbor instead. The winds were light, but the currents were with us, so we managed to sail using only the jenny through the archipelago of islands to reach Echo Bay by dinner time. We were entertained along the way by a fledgling eagle being coaxed to fly by a somewhat impatient mother.

Echo Bay was quiet. The Shadowfax shared the docks with only one other vessel until the large Coast Guard ship arrived to hunker down out of the weather for the evening. So, we weren't the only ones worried about the weather.

Have to admit there are definite advantages to this early season business. First, we don't have to fight over the washing machine and the dryer. During the height of the boating season last year we had to guard our places in line. The machines are the same ones from last year, with the same "Out of Order" sign on the second dryer and the loud banging sounds from the rust-coated washers while spinning. They work great however, so we have no complaints.

Another early season benefit is that we don't need reservations for dock space. We can pick any spot we want, and we don't have to wait in line for fuel either. Birds and wildlife have snuck back into the area for the off-season, and without loud boat engines or noisy generators running to camouflage the sounds, the echoing calls can be fully appreciated. In addition, this quiet morning we had the undivided attention of the Canadian Coast Guard for any emergencies that might come up.

We attempted a repeat of last year's 55-pound halibut catch, but didn't even get a nibble in front of Echo Bay. We tried Lagoon Cove's recommended tackle along with the obligatory "WATT Salmon Tails" saved and frozen from last year's salmon run at Stuart Island in the San Juan Islands of Washington State. The tails were to bring us luck, but didn't, at least at this particular point in time. Not to worry though—the tails would be refrigerated and re-used until we either catch something or the smell becomes too gross. I wonder if the tackle recommendations were driven by performance or profit from the sale of the product?

I know the Grand Banks "Armada" we encountered in Shoal Bay spent the previous evening at Lagoon before heading north because I was able to locate their blog on the internet to spy on their progress. Since we are traveling the same way only at a slower pace, I figure it would be helpful to see where they find open fuel and grocery facilities that we also can make use of. Their boat is called the Symphony and they last posted several days ago, so they may not have internet access where they are currently. It would be interesting to compare the success of the Shadowfax's aircard internet access to their state of the art satellite access.

Journal Entry #08
Sullivan Bay
May 23 & 24, 2006
The Broughtons

After leaving Echo Bay, we had an exhilarating sail up the channel to Sullivan Bay using just the jenny…which only got away from us once in a strong gust of wind, twirling the halyards together in a single tangled strand. At this point we reefed the jenny and it made all the difference in the world, changing the Shadowfax from a heel of 35 degrees to a more sedate 20 degrees. We also discovered that the sink in the head spews water all over the counter and floor at this angle. Fortunately, the toilet doesn't have the same problem.

Dan was the hero, saving the poor dingy "Shadow" from being swamped in the waves as it skated behind the Shadowfax on its painter. I think the dingy has decided to commit suicide by drowning rather than another planned escape as it did last year in Wellbore Channel.

Last year, in all the excitement of an exhilarating first time sail along Wellbore Channel, we managed to lose our dingy. It broke the painter (that's sailor talk for rope) and made a break for freedom. Unfortunately for the dingy, it was apprehended by another boater who contacted the Coast Guard with an animated discussion on the airwaves about who belonged to the dingy. I told Captain Bob we should name the dingy "Sheepish" instead of "Shadow."

We arrived at Sullivan Bay to find the Grand Banks "Armada" still in port due to the wind and poor weather reports. After two days at the docks, they were glad to see new faces and we were invited to their "Happy Hour." I think we were rather a curiosity to them, and we answered a lot of questions as to where our home port was, where we were going, and our plans for the summer. Captain Bob had fun telling them that we deliberately planned two short days so as not to catch up to the group in our sailboat because we figured there would be no dock space or diesel left. We were able to buy diesel though—even though it was $5.00 per gallon. Thank goodness we have a sailboat with a 35 gallon tank and we use less than one gallon per hour when under power.

We were told by one gentleman that people who own Grand Banks have more pride in their vessels than other boaters. Perhaps instead of "Armada," we should call them a "Pride" of boats. (Dan came up with that figure of speech.)

We were impressed by the planning of this group. They had their own captain and mechanic along and they had a weatherman contact on the East Coast of the United States. They had a definite schedule and probably group reservations at marinas along the route, so this delay was problematic for them. They also had a celebrity on board…Margo Woods, author of *Charlie's Charts*. She was gracious enough to autograph our copy of her book. She's a charming and friendly lady.

So now we have two books signed by their authors: *The Lagoon Cove Cookbook* signed by Bill, and *Charlie's Charts* signed by Margo. All we need now is the author of *Passage to Juneau* to sign his book for us!

Afterward, we felt like we had to try our luck at fishing again, so Captain Bob, Dan, Raeann, and I headed out in the Shadow to make a dent in the rockfish population of the area. Captain Bob caught a couple of little guys which he threw back to get bigger. We enjoyed the wonderful scenery until a tremendous downpour started. That's when we realized how far we were from the Shadowfax. We got so wet that we stopped worrying about sheltering body parts from the dampness and simply endured the rain. The water ran down inside our unmentionables, pants, hats, coats, and into our shoes. It rained so hard that the surface of the bay appeared to be dancing with globules of raindrops. Thank goodness for the clothes dryers at Sullivan Bay—all of our clothes, even coats and shoes went into the machines as soon as we peeled them off on the docks. We had to bail out the half submerged Shadow and even found water in the supposedly airtight compartments of the dingy. So, we had a fitting welcome to the North Coast.

Journal Entry #09
Cape Caution
May 24, 2006

We retired the Evergreen Pacific Cruising Atlas from Queen Charlotte Sound to Olympia since we passed the territory covered by its charts and are entering an area with names like Skull Cove, Fury Cove, Radar Passage, Gnarled Islets, Savage Island, and Safety Cove. We are traveling with jenny only, again accompanied by wind squalls that send us heeling and cabin items sliding to the floor. These must be the higher gusts promised in the forecast with the precise, emotionless pronunciation of the computerized forecaster. Small craft, gale, storm warnings—all issued in a cheerful, and sometimes sultry female voice.

The evergreen trees on the shoreline appear to point in unison towards one direction, apparently combed into place by the prevailing winds. Bleached tree trunks stab upwards, lower branches torn off by storms with only the green upper branches showing evidence of life. Trees on the small rock islands scattered about are sparse and scraggly trunks pointing every way the wind could possibly blow. It's a Van Gogh rugged landscape if ever I saw one.

We cautiously entered Takush Harbor and for the second time, found ourselves to be alone in a harbor. Alone except for the seals, loons, ducks, seagulls and a lone penguin (spotted by Raeann, who later acknowledged it could have been a cormorant).

The rain continues to follow us from Sullivan Bay and the Shadowfax has sprung a few deck leaks, which we have pans under. I don't consider this a major problem because it is raining so hard that it is equivalent to being upside down in the water. The deck was never made to become bottom-of-the-boat watertight. This might become an issue if it continues, but the folks at Sullivan Bay said this type of rain was highly unusual for this time of year. "This is winter kind of rain," they said. I think that was to make us feel better about the deluge.

The weather is supposed to improve tomorrow. We're supposed to see partial sun with light drizzle. After a breakfast of blueberry pancakes, scrambled eggs, and bacon, topped off with tomato juice cocktail, we pulled anchor and headed out of Smith Sound to the straits. We are less than two hours from Rivers Inlet and its supposed wealth of good fishing, so how could we not try our luck at fishing again?

We have settled into a pattern of waking at 6:00 A.M., making tea, coffee, and cocoa—which we consume in our bunks, then we get up for breakfast and the start of another day of travel.

Our gear has found resting places around the boat in these first few weeks of travel. Our hats rest on a "hat tree" made from the metal handhold in the salon with clothespins used as clips to hold the hats. A lone onion swings in state in a small hammock under the charts. The small electric fan that came with the Shadowfax is clipped on the chain plate support waiting for dinner and the next opportunity to vent cooking steam out the hatch. The guitar, computer printer, spinnaker, gale sail, and homemade riding sail are creatively bungeed securely on the salon shelving. Books with titles such as *Aground!, How to Cope with Storms, Boatowner's Mechanical and Electrical Manual, Understanding Weatherfax, GPS for Mariners, Navigation Rules and, Greatest Sailing Stories Ever Told* are tucked behind railings. Cups, plates, and pans are securely stowed behind teak racks. Nooks and crannies behind the salon seating are packed with dehydrated foods and baking supplies. Emergency repair equipment is stuffed under floorboards and back lockers. And of course, we have the old standbys: JB Weld, duct tape, and epoxy glue.

Journal Entry #10
Internet Access
May 25, 2006
Cape Caution North and Back Again

Broadband internet access from Seattle to Desolation Sound by aircard, laptop, booster, and antenna has been very reliable so far. At Sullivan Bay, the Shadowfax had the first instance of "service denied." Somehow I believe it's a conflict between Wi-Fi and aircard because I had a similar problem in Nanaimo. Both Sullivan Bay and Nanaimo have a strong Wi-Fi broadcast to the dock areas. I could work around the Nanaimo conflicts, but I couldn't get a connection at Sullivan Bay.

Leaving my laptop on while running up the coastline, I could watch the aircard's access light going from green to red as we traveled in and out of coverage areas. As long as there is coverage, the speeds are DSL-like, very acceptable for usage. Some of the green bars indicated coverage was available, but not evidently through Verizon or their partner, Telus, because of the "service denied" signals that were generated. Either that, or our signal was too weak to have the towers respond.

I plan to chart the aircard access bars and internet speed during our trip north. I figure this information will be useful for a year or so—at least until new towers and technology come along. I'm thinking that we need to publish a *Watt Internet Access Cruising Guide*—it might be a best seller.

May 26, 2006

This morning we sailed up Fitzhugh Sound in sunshine with a reefed main and jenny. The aircard got a weak signal at the base of Calvert Island, then nothing, not even the tiny green blip that means there is potential access. We are heading up a narrow passageway with a rather exotic name—Kwakshua Channel—that cuts across the island to Queen Charlotte Sound. Pruth Bay will be our anchorage for the evening. In the morning we plan to sail up and around Hecate Island to Hakai Pass.

We have no internet access at Pruth Bay or Hakai Pass. I would be suspicious of my equipment, except the cell phones are also non-functional. Perhaps we'll have better luck as we get closer to Bella Bella.

May 31, 2006
Approach to Prince Rupert

Still no internet access or phone! I am a little disappointed, but since the aircard worked so well up to Cape Caution, I can't complain. I understand there is broadband access at the dock at Prince Rupert. We are hoping to stay there, so I can probably get online then. Bella Bella was supposed to have a large new cellular presence, but it wasn't up and running yet. A large block of this coast is still unavailable to cell phone and broadband aircard access.

June 1, 2006 Prince Rupert

Well the Prince Rupert Yacht Club has internet access, but you have to rent a piece of hardware called a "hub" and load a program onto your computer that might override anything else. We passed on the rental and download. There is an internet café nearby and free Wi-Fi internet at the Breakers Restaurant next to the yacht club, so we have options to surf the net without the aircard access. I am not sure what the problem with access is at Prince Rupert—it is perhaps analog only and both the cell phones and aircard are digital. Jordan Kellogg of Verizon Wireless emailed me a Telus (Verizon's partner in Canada) coverage map. It indicated coverage in Prince Rupert, but both cell phone and aircard could not gain access to the system.

June 3, 2006
US Waters, near Mary Island entering Ketchikan area Alaska

A tantalizing whiff of internet access near Mary Island—the aircard light acts the same way as at Cape Caution where my last access was available. Should start working.

June 4 & 5, 2006
Ketchikan 55.20.30 N, 131.38.59 W

Good internet access at Thomas Basin—over 417 K until the cruise ships arrive, then speed is affected by their use of the system. Got excellent internet reception in the Tongass Channel.

June 6-12, 2006
Wrangell

We sailed up the back passages to Wrangell, but we still didn't have aircard internet access. And we didn't have aircard or Wi-Fi access at the Wrangell docks either. It is possible to pay to use the desktop connection available at a store near the dock.

June 13- 14, 2006
Petersburg

No aircard Wi-Fi dock access except for a hot spot provider that charges by the day or year. The hotspot (Hotspot AK) is in the Petersburg harbormaster office area. The library has free internet usage on their machines and the town has some pay by the minute desktops available.

June 15-21, 2006
Clarence Strait

No internet access from Clarence Strait south to Coffman Cove. Thorne Bay dock is advertised as a hotspot, but we had no such luck. The libraries in Coffman Cove and Thorne Bay might have provided access if they would have been open.

June 24, 2006
North of Ketchikan

There has been an improvement in reception since we last traveled across Clarence Strait northbound from Ketchikan. Last time we just had access to the end of Tongass Channel, now we have access at the end of Cleveland Island in Clarence Strait, across from the Kasaan Pennisula.

June 25, 2006
Hassler Harbor (south of Ketchikan) 55.12.86 N, 131.25.68 W

Still good internet coverage (5 bars) in harbor.

June 26-July 7, 2006 NO AIRCARD ACCESS

We haven't had any aircard access in: Hartley Bay, Prince Rupert (dock Wi-Fi only), Grenville Channel, Butedale, Knxeal Inlet, Khutz Inlet, Bishop Bay, Bolin Bay, Kynock Bay, or Fiordland.

July 8, 2006
Return to Bella Bella/Shearwater

New broadband internet has been activated here going from Bella Bella (at 829 K) south to Lama Passage to Twilight Point where just two or three bars are available at 52.05.170 N and 128.05.564 W. According to the local folks, internet access was activated in the last week. Very exciting!

July 14, 2006
Cape Caution

Started getting internet access south of Cape Caution. Rocking of the boat and large swells seem to affect continuous access. Finally we got firm access at 51.04.673 N, 127.48.974 W in Queen Charlotte Straits. Speed is 714 K.

July 20, 2006
Allies Island, Desolation Sound 50.12.57 N, 124.48.45 W

We only get two bars here, but when I connect as I do sporadically, it is at 234 K. I have noticed that when the connection is weak, even gentle rocking of the boat will disconnect the signal. Probably this is what happened at Cape Caution in the swell and waves when I had a signal. This is an issue to remember when mounting an antenna. We have ours on the rail and thought a mast mount would be a better option. We may have to rethink this idea.

This is the end of the internet access report. It would be interesting to compare internet accessibility in these areas as technology improves.

Journal Entry #11
Raven Steals the Camera
May 27, 2006
West Beach, Hakai Pass

The Shadowfax spent a quiet evening alone at anchor in Pruth Bay. We anchored in front of the Hakai Resort which is still closed for the season. It's abandoned except for two young caretakers and a lonely young black cat. That cat wanted to go with us in the worst possible way, weaving itself around our ankles and following us along the hiking trail to West Beach. When it got far enough from the resort to become uncomfortable it stopped, then wailed in misery because we continued on without him. I heard the caretakers call the cat "Crab Bait," so there may have been a reason it was so desperate to leave the island with us.

West Beach was unexpected in its beauty and grandeur. It had at least a mile of uninhabited sandy beaches and the ocean swells that weaved their way around the rocky islets in the large bay were something to see. White cliffs with bonsai trees and bushes formed a green top coat that oozed and dribbled along the crevices. Eagles, seabirds, and ravens soared over the kelp beds looking for dinner. The camera couldn't catch the perspective and the essence of the scene, so we left it along with coats, shoes and socks on the huge driftwood logs cast up on the upper portions of the beach.

We wandered for an hour or two admiring the views, enjoying the feel of water between our toes as we collected shells in the sunshine. It was a magical experience! As we headed back, a large raven soared past us just over our heads—so near we could see the expression in his eyes. Ravens are normally suspicious and shy around humans so it was surprising to see him at this close range. Of course, I didn't have my camera.

When we got back to the pile of our belongings, it looked as if a tiny tornado had touched down—shoes and coats were scattered, socks were cast down the beach, and my camera (the one we are using to record our travels) was tumbled onto the sand, lens cap off, dials turned, and covered with sand.

The culprit turned out to be a raven—his birdie footprints told the tale in the sand as he had attempted to make off with the fascinating, shiny, possibly edible camera. Good thing the camera was too heavy for him.

Journal Entry #12
Bella Bella
May 28, 2006
Shearwater Bay Dock

There is a definite demarcation from an absence to an abundance of feed fish with its associated increase in predators at Bella Bella. Herring and perch form fishy blankets under the docks, allowing locals to "rake" for fishing bait. Eagles have become commonplace and perch close to the dock fish cleaning stations offering exceptional photo opportunities of fish theft from unwitting fishermen. We enjoyed ourselves by placing freshly caught perch on the docks to have eagles snatch them even before our backs were turned. The video camera caught the sound of the eagle's talons hitting the dock with a clunk as it took the fish.

Local fisherman claim that halibut can be caught anywhere in the area in which a one hundred and fifty foot underwater ledge exists. We will have to test this theory with the rockfish carcasses left over from our fishing in Hakai Pass. The weather has been exceptional and we want to push further north towards Prince Rupert to make as much progress as possible before the rain starts again, so our fishing may be limited.

Raeann has turned into super fisherwoman, hanging off the bow of the Shadowfax in seven foot swells while fishing. "The Scopolamine Kid" has come a long way since she boarded the Shadowfax in Meydenbauer Bay loaded with seasick medications and headache remedies!

Journal Entry #13
Song of the Shadowfax
May 28, 2006
Klemtu

Today was a full day of sailing from Bella Bella to Klemtu across Milbank Sound accompanied by some southeasterly breezes. Both Raeann and I spent a large portion of the day snoozing in the warmth of the cabin, leaving the sailing (and the misty-cold fog) to the men. We coasted along with the wind, sails wing on wing, riding up and down the large swells from the open ocean.

The Shadowfax creates a song as she sails—the topping lift that taps rhythmically against the mast accompanied by the faster beating of the two flag halyards. Both sounds gain in intensity and tempo with larger gusts of wind, then, subside as the wind slows. Water slides and burbles against the hull, interspersed, with wave slaps. The winches make a clanging and whirring sound as they are cranked to tighten and loosen the jenny and there are gentle shifting sounds as the boat hull takes up the strain with different tacks. Ropes slither over the decks, sometimes with large, not-so-rhythmic thumps when they catch and then suddenly release. The Shadowfax is not a silent sailor!

Amid gale warnings, we anchored in a small cove just inside the start of Klemtu Passage, the start of our long trek up Tolmie Channel and Grenville Channel. We will eventually reach Prince Rupert in 140 nautical miles and feel relieved that we have reached protected passageways before this big blow.

Our evening entertainment was again due to a local eagle, chasing his dinner. In this case a full grown Canadian goose was the eagle's target. The goose was easily able to evade the eagle and kept up an indignant honking commentary during the whole chase. The presence of eagles indicated the possibility of fish in the area, so Raeann got out her fishing pole with a small white rubber worm for bait. The watched became the watcher as the hungry eagle spent quite a bit of time observing Raeann's fishing attempts in the hope she would provide a fishy dinner for him to steal. Suddenly we all heard the reel line screaming and a wail from Raeann "Could I get some help out here?" With much grunting, groaning, and luck, she finally pulled in a twenty four pound halibut.

The eagle did finally get a meal after Captain Bob cleaned the catch. As soon as the fish entrails were dumped into the water, the eagle swooped, grabbed, and carried them off. From now on we will refer to this moorage as "Raeann's Cove," or perhaps "Halibut Gut Bay."

Our meals have been excellent (from all the crew's reports). I learned from last year's first voyage and am now a seasoned boat cook. What could be better than homemade apple pies, ginger cookies, fried cod, bean sprout salad, vanilla lattes, blueberry pancakes, and now halibut roasts and steaks?

I can't take full credit for the food preparation though. My sister, who is my twin, is a seasoned sailor. She sails the Chesapeake, the Bahamas, the Caribbean, Europe—you get the picture. She knows about sailboats and food stuff so she was full of good advice when I asked about what our needs might be. As a result, I immediately alienated our UPS delivery guy when my first order of dehydrated and canned goods arrived fresh off the internet site recommended by my twin. He stacked up huge boxes of food in front of our front door blocking all entry and informed me he would not be delivering all these items to our front door in the future.

I had ordered all the wonderful things displayed on this special website—dried corn, potatoes, peas, green beans, peppers, onions, eggs, broccoli, apples, strawberries, eggs etc. What an amazing thing to realize that almost everything you can purchase fresh in a grocery store you can also purchase dehydrated. Canned meats and cheeses were also available, and as my sister highly recommended these items, I also made sure I purchased canned goods. What I didn't comprehend is the difference between a number two and a half can and a number 10 can. Turns out that those numbers are sizes and 10 is the largest size you can buy. Somehow, I missed this lesson in Home Economics, so we have enough food to last for a long time. Good thing this stuff lasts for years.

Some of the food prior to reconstitution looks pretty recognizable. Not so the broccoli and green beans. If we are ever boarded by the Coast Guard and they find my stash of broccoli and green beans, I'm thinking I'll have a lot of explaining to do.

Journal Entry #14
The Heart Shaped Garden
May 30, 2006
Butedale, Inside Passage

From Klemtu we headed up Tolmie Channel, hoping to reach Bishop Bay's hot springs, but the Shadowfax had other plans. Two hours into our run, the gauges and voltage regulator indicated a serious problem, which meant we couldn't continue to charge from our engine alternator. This is the same issue we had in 2005, except that back then, the brand new alternator destroyed itself in 62 hours and was replaced under Westerbeke's engine warranty. Too bad they didn't replace the regulator at that time since it seems to be the source of our electrical problem.

So, we were 120 miles from any repair parts and in full energy conservation mode. No water pumping, lights, GPS, or heat unless absolutely necessary. All battery power had to be saved to run the engine. We had sails, but the wind was non-existent.

That being the case, we lay over at Butedale, which is on the way to Prince Rupert. The large waterfall welcomed us into the bay and we were able to tie up to a dilapidated dock, the floating remnants of a large cannery village, now abandoned except for an elderly caretaker, an old dog, and possibly an older cat. There were quite a few large buildings: a former two-story hotel, a dormitory or bunkhouse, a store, a few homes, a washhouse, and a laundry building that was on pilings—half collapsed into the bay. All had moss covered roofs. Some had trees growing out of the shingles, and a lonely fire hydrant stood in state in the half-mowed grassy area in the center of the buildings. Electrical wires were strung haphazardly between the buildings, power provided by the single automotive alternator attached to the old generator pulley at the waterfall. Debris littered the area and there were piles of collapsed stairs, old boilers, and cannery machinery laying half in and out of the saltwater. All around I could see barely legible peeling signs optimistically promising ice cream and showers.

A number of old boats in different states of disrepair shared the moorage with the Shadowfax, the closest was an old blue fishing boat with a tremendous hole in the bow that had been patched with a nailed on sheet of plywood. As we arrived, the caretaker, named Lou, was carefully scraping the blue paint off the side of this hulk. As he later told us proudly, the last owner gave him this vessel in exchange for $1000 and a ride to the nearest town. I would say the escaping owner got the best part of the bargain.

There was something incongruous between the meticulous scraping of the old hull and the surrounding scene of disrepair and neglect. Another newer boat moored nearby was also in keeping with its surroundings, called the Miss Jean. Its superstructure had been damaged by winter storms and looked most un-seaworthy.

The harbor is reminiscent of the old native villages that were slowly abandoned over time with possibly an old caretaker to welcome passersby until no one stopped anymore and the villages disappeared. In comparison to the native villages that vanish without a trace other than a midden on the beach, this village will leave permanent marks on the landscape. The metal boilers, water tanks, concrete foundations, and the piping for power generation will remain long after Lou has left.

Lou has mowed the yards around some of the buildings and a small, plastic covered greenhouse along with a minimal garden are a testimonial to his tenacity in his lonely vigil at Butedale. There are rhubarb, potatoes, and perhaps beans and peas sprouting in patches out of surprisingly rich, dark soil. One garden bed set aside from the small vegetable growing area has been carefully weeded with its edges marked with small stones, and the bare dirt center sculpted into the shape of a mounded heart. To symbolize Miss Jean? Lost dreams? Or perhaps a final grasp at beauty and repair to contrast with the desolation of the ruins.

According to Lou, the white "Spirit Bear" visits Butedale occasionally, he mentioned he had seen it May 4, about a month prior, on the beach near the old pilings. Our skepticism vanished when fellow travelers from a fishing boat hiked up to the lake above to fish and came back with tales of white bear sightings that evening. Perhaps on our way back down to Seattle we will stop at Butedale again and have another chance to see this mythical creature.

Journal Entry #15
Kxngeal Inlet
May 31, 2006
Grenville Channel

We spent the night in a wonderful cove off of Grenville Channel, approximately 40 miles from Prince Rupert. The bay is unpronounceable and we were alone except for two eagles, some seals, and a number of river otters all either eating dinner, or attempting to.

Because of her previous fishing success, Raeann spent the evening fishing for more halibut. We decided that this must be a halibut nursery, because all that was caught were the tiny cousins of halibut—little sole or flounder. This bay has a small river entering at its end and the resulting silt has built up into a delta of mud and sand that make for excellent habitat for these fishy creatures. The anchoring gets a little tricky, however, because the delta shoals so abruptly. We watched the Shadowfax swing on its anchor line and saw the depth sounder display go unnervingly from 112 feet to 12 feet and back again.

Snow covered mountains formed a halo around the Shadowfax and we fell asleep to the sound of water pouring down from the streams on the hillsides. It was a quiet and uneventful night despite anchoring irregularities.

(The familiarity of this cove was welcome on our return voyage as it provided a known safe harbor from some unexpectedly strong winds in Grenville Channel.)

Journal Entry #16
Five Nautical Miles from Alaska
June 3, 2006
Goose Bay, Dundas Island

The Shadowfax arrived at Prince Rupert on June 1. We did laundry, shopping, engine repairs, and continued on our way the following day. Prince Rupert was the home of eagles. Dozens of seemingly tame eagles had made the local fishing boat garbage dumpsters their hangout for breakfast, lunch, and dinner. Eagles of all ages and associated plumage perched on the docks, dumpsters, and on rocky beaches vying for rotting fish carcasses.

Our crossing of Chatham Sound was uneventful and under power with light winds. As a result, we reached our evening moorage by 6:00 P.M. It was the harbor of Goose Bay—vacant except for a lone float, some fishing boats, and some sort of floating barge-house. The evening's entertainment was not due to eagles, but to some exasperated fishermen who were very unhappy with the 60-foot pleasure boat that had tied up to their private float. As we ate dinner in the salon, the verbiage that floated over the water got louder and louder, with f-words interspersed at frequent intervals.

The trespassing boat never left, but no one on the vessel had enough nerve to come above decks either. It sat at the float looking totally abandoned with no movement aboard it for the rest of the evening. We went to bed early tonight, knowing we had a long run tomorrow to get to Ketchikan and U.S. Customs, but our sleep was interrupted a number of times during the night. The first problem was the long daylight hours—it was light until at least 11:00 P.M. Then at about 1:00 or 2:00 A.M., a spotlight flashed over the Shadowfax and we got out of bed to investigate. A very large vessel was shining a bright spotlight from outside the harbor, casting light over all the anchored boats and lighting up the shore. Coast Guard? Fishing boat? We never found out, and finally settled down to sleep again.

At maybe 2:30 or 3:00 A.M., a strange wind came up. There seems to be an odd wind that comes up in this area—it starts as a whisper, a gentle whooshing noise that increases to a groan or moan, shaking the rigging and halyards hard, but leaving the waters calm, and with cool air chilling the cabin. The wind moans and blows for a while and then silently disappears. Very eerie, and probably the source of some Haida stories. I will have to research what ghostly entity visited us during the night.

Journal Entry #17
The Stairs of Ketchikan
June 4-6, 2006
Alaska

As we got closer to the Alaskan Port of Ketchikan, we could see the many tall white buildings enclosing the harbor—surprisingly massive structures for a smallish fishing town. Motoring a little closer up Revillagigedo Channel, we were made aware of our mistake, not skyscrapers, cruise ships! All of them white with many stories, festooned with orange life-rafts and precise balconies. We saw four mammoth ships at the docks and anchored out in the bay.

As we got closer, another thing stood out, the stairs. Old Ketchikan is built on rocks and cliffs, houses are sometimes on pilings, sometimes on rock, but always have stairs—Dr. Seuss type stairs—going up, up, up, continuing up, and winding around. Truly amazing. I can't imagine using those stairs in an icy winter.

If Prince Rupert was the home of the eagles, then Ketchikan has to be the home of the raven. Magnificent birds congregated in the harbor checking out the commercial fishing boats for potential snacks of fish, crab, and unattended lunches left out by unwary crew members. We tempted a few birds with a peanut butter sandwich, but they ignored our offering until our backs were turned, then the sandwich silently vanished.

We tied to a dock in the boat basin and headed for the town to look it over. Ketchikan has had a colorful past with bordellos filled with gold miners and fishermen. The buildings are still there—some repaired for the tourist trade, others closed up with "For Sale" or "Closed" or "For Rent" posted prominently. Gold still is an important commodity for the city, however, not as in gold nuggets and mining, but as in jewelry stores that sell their products to the cruise line tourists in the summer. Their signs proclaim connections to stores in the Caribbean, which makes sense if you contemplate the international aspect of the cruise ship lines which own a lot of these stores. Summer in Alaska, winter in the Caribbean!

The tourists descend and ascend these vast ships like the creatures depicted in the biblical story of Noah's Ark. They are lined up, counted, identified, tagged, and sorted. The tour buses are packed so tightly that the gaze of passengers attempting to view the scenery is blocked by fogged glass windows. Some riders attempted to wipe a circular spot to see through, but it was a futile effort with all the humid air. Watching the buses pass with their victims encased inside made me feel relieved to be on the smaller cruise ship and the itinerary of the Shadowfax.

The cruise lines have constructed new docks, buildings, and stores that seem to have sucked the life from the older shopping areas. Wonderful old buildings with elaborate storefronts sit empty with peeling paint and rotting wood, ignored by the invaders who focus on the newer and "improved" stores of the cruise lines.

Some local residents have a kind of resentment about the cruise lines and how they have taken over the summer scene. We were treated to a long diatribe about the cruise lines and money laundering in Ketchikan by one of the owners of a small business by the docks. Businesses proudly proclaim they are "privately owned" with signs on storefronts and cash registers.

The town is flooded with tourists when the ships come in during the day, at night the boats whisk everyone away and the town becomes vacant again. The fishing docks once more are the center of activity.

As we left Ketchikan, motoring up Tongass Narrows, it was hard not to feel a little bit like a target. The port is an important seaplane hub for Alaska, and planes were taking off every couple of minutes—some loaded so heavily it took them a long time to get off the water and that worried me a little. The Shadowfax mast sticks up 60 feet in the air and those seaplanes seemed to fly pretty close. I am sure they missed by hundreds of feet, but there was no evading those planes and the fear of collision they inspired. They swarmed in and out of the harbor like yellow jackets whose nest has been poked by a stick.

This is were Dan and Raeann left the Shadowfax and returned home. From now on the Shadowfax would continue her adventures with a crew of two.

Journal Entry #18
Santa Anna Inlet
June 8 & 9, 2006
North of Ketchikan

We spent two days in this wonderful harbor. This is the Alaska Wilderness we came to see! Waterfalls tumbling down steep wooded slopes to serenade our moorage, sunshine, a lake to hike to—eagles fishing…the only thing missing is the bears! The end of the inlet has a large stream connected to Lake Helen, about a quarter of a mile from the bay, and large schools of perch as thick as herring balls line the edges of the shore near the fresh water. The eagles and seals must think of this as their "McDonalds."

Traveling up the coast, the eagles have become more and more numerous and the opportunity to watch them has given us new insight about their behavior. In the San Juan Islands, eagles are wary and sparse, but here they abound. They are more opportunistic than I had imagined. They snatch small and large fish, and even steal fish from unsuspecting victims. An eagle attempted such a feat about ten feet from the side of the Shadowfax as we motored away from Ketchikan. I am not sure if the eagle had the fish first, or if the seal snatched the fish from the eagle, but I suspect the latter was the case. We got a great view of a madly thrashing eagle valiantly attempting to drag the fish and seal away for dinner. The seal held on as the eagle flapped its wings, pulling with such force that the seal's grey body surfed along behind until the eagle lost its grip and flew off.

We were not alone in this harbor either night. The first night we had two remnants of the Grand Banks "Pride" anchored near us, probably heading back south after the big rendezvous at Wrangell. The next night a solitary power cruiser, not a Grand Banks, shared the bay with us.

The only other company in the bay was the ruins of an old cannery or mining operation—much like Butedale will probably look in a hundred years or so, only on a smaller scale. Boilers lay submerged and intertwined with old pilings on the rocky beach. Rusty crankshafts and water pipes littering the area told a tale of futile efforts to carve a commercially viable niche.

The forest covered over any cleared areas. Only the beaches cleared of rocks or heaped of rocks in organized fashions showed that man has been there. The natives made rock "clam gardens" that neatly lined the beaches. The immigrating whites made rock piles to support their structures. The organization of stones remain, but both peoples are gone.

Journal Entry #19
The Promyshlenniki of Berg Bay
June 10, 2006
Wrangell Area

Promyshlenniki (pronounced pro-meesh'le-eekee) was a Russian term used to describe a lawless group of Siberian fur-trading thugs known for drunkenness, avarice, and vicious cruelty around the time of Peter the Great. They descended upon the Aleutian Islands and Alaska after the discovery of the valuable furs by early explorers. I think we may have met some of their descendants staying at a forest service cabin in Berg Bay.

We started our motor sail from Santa Anna Inlet and worked our way toward some spectacular inside passageways surrounded by snow covered mountains. The scale here is vast and we are finding that distances are very deceiving. Traveling from one inlet to another takes a much longer travel time than it should based solely on visual observations. We have to keep counting out the nautical miles on the charts or GPS. Mountains are big. Creeks are big. Tides are really big. Even the bears are big. I filmed two Brown Bears (grizzlies?) sunning themselves on a beach as we passed. When Captain Bob told me they were grizzlies, the images jumped up and down reflecting my excitement. I must have some Italian in me because I can't talk excitedly and not gesture with my hands at the same time—a bad habit for someone who wants to take good video cinematography.

We reached Berg Bay—yet another sunny, magical place. We anchored and went for a dingy exploration a few miles up the Aaron Creek Delta. We did fine until the tide went out. The deep water we had motored up was no longer deep enough to motor, so we rowed, then, poled our way out to the river's mouth again. Good thing it wasn't a low tide or we would have been walking on the river bottom dragging the dingy along.

At our anchorage we found we had been joined by a couple more boats—expensive twin red and white American Tugs (made in La Conner, WA) who tied up to the forest service float in the harbor. Our guide book said not to tie to these floats as they went with the cabin and were rented out. After what transpired later in the evening, nothing could induce us to violate that admonition.

We settled in for a leisurely Friday night enjoying the setting sun on the mountainous peaks around us, when a small outboard skiff with an irate Alaskan came barreling into the harbor at full speed. Words were exchanged with the tugboats about usage of the float, but the tugboats refused to budge. The skiff took off again at full tilt out of the bay and left us rocking and rolling. Our quiet evening was over. The Alaskan returned with reinforcements and the rest of his camping and hunting party, with all the ferrying trips made at full wake speed.

Soon shouts filled the bay, coming from the vicinity of the shore where camp was being set up by the hunters. We overheard the hunter's loud comments about the opening of bear hunting season, and shortly afterwards target practice commenced. Gunshots echoed around the bay, a few sporadic bursts, a volley of 20 rounds, then silence. All this noise resonated and bounced from the mountains surrounding us, the resultant effect scaring away any potential targets. We hoped the bears we had seen earlier were long gone, since they wouldn't have stood a chance against these drive-by-boat-shooters.

This wasn't the end of the disruptions. The same group of hunters built a bonfire and the partying started. People were drinking, laughing, singing, shouting, and shooting off guns until darkness settled in after midnight. Somebody shouted out over the bay, "Anybody want to party?"

I don't think there were any takers.

Journal Entry #20
Jet Boats of the Stikine River
June 11 & 12, 2006
Wrangell Harbor

We arrived in Wrangell on Saturday at 5:00 P.M. to find all the gas docks and stores closed for the evening. Everyone was off salmon fishing for the big weekend derby. We tied up at the transient's dock and prepared to wait for Monday when fuel and groceries would be available again.

The town shuts down on Sunday, but not the tour boats. We talked to an operator the next morning and decided to take a jet boat trip up the huge Stikine River Delta that stretches 330 miles north of Wrangell. We had 10 minutes to throw together lunch, bug spray, sunscreen, hats, sunglasses, cameras, and coats before surrendering $179 dollars each for a six hour ride. What a boat! Twin 351 Fords with two matching Hamilton jet drives pushing a 28-foot aluminum boat made for the Hells Canyon boating areas of Idaho. I watched the tachometer and noted that in open water we cruised at 40 mph, while in the shallower river areas the average speed was 30 mph. A lot of the time, even at these speeds, the depth sounder showed no reading because it was too shallow (the guide said he couldn't slow down or he would get *stuck*?).

The Stikine River area makes the Skagit River of Washington State area look like a veritable dribble of water. The Stikine is vast—surrounded by 5,000 foot snow covered mountains and glaciers all feeding snowmelt into the tributaries that form the grand river. The delta itself fans out and covers about 15 square nautical miles. It covers about a quarter of the chart's area. A lot of that delta is not navigatible because it is too shallow and parts are dry at low tide, such as the descriptively named Dry Straits. Jet drives, canoes, or kayaks, are the only option of travel in these areas.

We crisscrossed the many canals heading up the river until we, the passengers, couldn't tell north from south or even where we had started our wild ride into the mountains. We saw stranded icebergs that were 40-feet thick stuck on sandbars and we even collected blue ice for our evening cocktails. We finally met the state bird of Alaska—the mosquito, during our "rest" stops along the way on the muskeg. There isn't enough insect repellant in the world for these guys. The guide offered up the electric bug zapper. We took turns flailing at the mosquitoes that hitchhiked in the boat as we twisted and turned at full speed in the narrow canals.

Wrangell is a wonderful town with about 1,500 inhabitants and all are friendly. The town has the flavor of what I remember of the small town in Ohio in the 1950's where I spent a few early years. Everyone greets each other in passing; children ride bikes down the main street; teenagers swim, jump, and fish off the docks; the one ice cream store is packed with customers while other stores remain closed evenings and weekends; no malls; no apparent movie theatres; sparse vehicle traffic (and what there is always stops for pedestrians); and gaily decorated homemade booths being set up for the annual 4th of July celebrations (weeks in advance since it is such a big event for the town). Teenagers are recruited to help parents run their stores and seem to do so cheerfully, glad for the opportunity to earn money.

Instead of hot rods, teenagers and adults have hot boats—small skiffs sporting over-sized outboard engines with no mufflers. We saw the boats running wide open from dawn until dusk in the waters in front of Wrangell Harbor.

Dusk isn't until nearly midnight, and dawn starts shortly thereafter. Ready to move to Wrangell? You should probably know that the annual rainfall in the Wrangell area is at least 82 inches a year, so you might want to give it a second thought.

Journal Entry #21
The Mossy Boats of Petersburg
June 13 & 14, 2006
Petersburg Harbor, Mitkof Island

Petersburg is a fishing town with a strong Norwegian heritage, with colorful Rosemaling decorating many of the buildings in the retail area. Sidewalks are not ignored in this Scandinavian art celebration. Fanciful brass inlays depicting marine fish and birds decorate many of the walking areas and the surrounding buildings are brightly painted. It is as if the colorful artwork attempts to detract from the depressing effects of the abundant year-around rain. With 109 inches per year, that is almost nine inches a month, roughly two inches a week, with most precipitation falling in the winter months.

We had the opportunity to explore the hillside above Petersburg and enjoyed the muskeg areas of small pines, moss, grasses, and marvelous wildflowers. The community has made mile-long boardwalks on the muskeg to allow hikers to savor the beauty and fragrance of this park-like area.

The fishing boats in the North Harbor area are fishing and crabbing boats—hard working vessels, some of which are live-a-boards, some of which contain shipshape transients waiting to head out, some are in the process of repair, and others are badly in need of repair. Fantastical tents have been constructed around some of these boats. They have blue or clear tarps and are tied with duct tape, bungee cords, rope, wire, and any other possible form of attachment in an attempt to ward off the effects of the rain. The boats moored without protection grow thick moss gardens on their hulls, cabins, windows, and engines—the moss oozing down in a thick green frosting. Grass and ferns sprout on the wood hulls of old seiners seemingly moored and abandoned, filled with debris and fascinating rusty parts. The fishy smell of the harbor permeates the air and any vessels moored therein participate by absorbing the odor.

Mooring the Shadowfax at the marina was a challenge, not due to the tight quarters next to all the fishing boats, but due to the antics of herring fishermen who were busy jigging in the harbor. These fishermen seem to be the same kind of fanatics that we get at Stuart Island during humpy (a type of salmon) fishing season—they totally ignore anything around them but the fish as they run their boats around in a mad herring school chase. Forty foot sailboats moving even at a sedate 1.2 knots have trouble slamming into reverse (or moving in any evasive direction) when a small skiff charges within feet of its bow. I understand that behavior over catching salmon, but herring?

These Petersburg fishermen are hardy. We saw people sitting in the cold rain in open skiffs fishing all day for salmon. They were properly attired in the standard Alaskan uniform of raingear: brown boots and life jackets, but it has to be freezing cold! It appeared to be the accepted form of fishing to sit exposed to the elements rather than in the warm shelter of a covered cabin. I guess it's the Alaskan way.

Journal Entry #22
Shadowfax Meets a Glacier
June 15 & 16, 2006
Thomas Bay, Alaska

The large bay to the north of Petersburg is the home to Baird and Patterson Glaciers, both of which are tidewater glaciers and as such do not give rise to icebergs. We spent our first night at Spray Island, one of the recommended anchorages in the bay, and then being more daring, the second night chose a non-recommended anchorage at Scenery Cove. Our guide book said the cove wasn't a good anchorage overnight, but we found a good hold in the mouth of the bay and did a shore tie.

This placed us within striking distance of our goal—the Baird Glacier and its tidal moraine just visible around the point from our anchorage. We planned to take the Shadowfax closer the next morning, but we couldn't stand not to explore in the Shadow (our dingy) and set off as soon as we could get our gear together: raincoats (it was raining hard) blankets (it was cold), handheld VHF (for emergency), fishing poles (cause you never know), and a bag to protect our camera gear.

As we approached the moraine, we found it only partially exposed. The tide was high and all the rounded boulders tumbled together in piles of differing heights and sizes. It was a monochromatic moonscape except for a few tufts of grass and the sound of seagulls. The moraine appeared to stretch about a mile to the start of the glacier which was bare except for some patches of leftover ice. This ice was dirty and had debris embedded in it and on the very top it had huge house-sized boulders, not rounded at all, but sharp and jutting upwards, probably plucked from the surrounding peaks as the glacier melted and receded.

We motored carefully up the opaque, silt-filled river with frequent downward stabs of our oar to check the depth, accompanied by soundings with a buzz-bomb. Strange ominous bubbles and belches were emitted from below as we moved up against the current as if we were being followed by unseen creatures.*

The water was cold. A mile away, at the Shadowfax moorage, the water temperature was 46 degrees, but here ice chunks floated in the current and the breeze from the glacier made snowfall feel imminent. We landed on the moraine and realized just how deceiving distances are in Alaska—what seemed to be a short stroll from the Shadowfax turned out to be an impossible hike. Pictures and more exploring would have to be postponed until tomorrow when we could get the Shadowfax closer. Leaving the moraine, we retraced our route out of the mouth of the river and headed back for the boat.

Did I mention tidewater glaciers don't have icebergs? They do, however, have huge ice pieces floating just under the surface that are invisible because of all the silt in the water. The poor Shadow hit one and knocked the outboard up. That was the bad news. The good news is that ice gives, so no damage was done or we would have had a long miserable row. We decided to keep the Shadowfax well away from the glacier.

When we returned to the Shadowfax, we found company moored nearby at the head of the cove—a fishing boat whose unusual name made us notice it in Petersburg. The name defined meant Wild Woman. Spying with binoculars in the bitter cold, we watched as two identically clad unisex crewmembers took kayaks and headed for shore and the river running out of it. As they climbed out of the kayaks and headed up the river to hunt for gold, fish, or maybe to picnic, it became evident that the smaller person was a young woman and the other person her beau. In the cold rain, wearing boots, raingear, and waders, they held hands as they walked through the wet mosquito filled muskeg. They were truly full-fledged Alaskan Sourdoughs!

This is Scenery Cove in Thomas Bay. It provided adequate anchorage despite dire anchorage reports in our guide.

* Later we read a book purchased in Ketchikan about Thomas Bay. The Native Americans referred to it as the "Bay of Death," and early gold miners called it the "Devil's Country," all due to the strange happenings associated with the area. Reputedly, devils lurking in the mountains lured prospectors to horrible deaths from madness and exposure to the elements.

Journal Entry #23
Alaskan Language
July 17, 2006
St John's Bay

Alaska has its own everyday language—a *sourdough* is either a yeast-dough mixture to cook with or a person who has spent most of his or her life in Alaska; *Petersburg sneakers, Sitka Slippers, and Ketchikan sneakers*—are brown rubbers boots worn year-round to every event; cheechako is a newcomer to Alaska; *termination dust* is the first snow on the mountains (at the end of summer); *dungie* is the nickname for dungeness crabs; *highliner* is a top producing commercial fishermen; *slime line* is the cleaning area around a cannery. And they have many more odd words.

I think they should add another one: Alaskan minefield. Not for gold, but for what happens when crabbing season gets underway and the Alaskan commercial dungeness fishermen set their pots out. These pots need to be placed in sheltered, mud bottomed bays with a depth of 40-70 feet. We awoke on the morning after crabbing season opened to find ourselves surrounded by crab pots in our bay. We managed to evade entanglement by placing a watch on the bow as we carefully evaded the pots, zigging and zagging our way out of the bay and into deeper portions of Wrangell Narrows.

We are finding that these crab pots are going to be a major issue for our anchoring, as there is nowhere left to anchor when these guys are done setting their pots. In St John's Bay we were forced to anchor on a questionable bottom near rocks and current because of this pot placement. We set up the GPS monitor to notify us if we moved beyond a certain radius—it worked great, but we were up a couple of times during the night when the raucous alarm sounded.

Southeast Alaska is called so because of its geographical location. Another reason might be for how often the weather person on the radio uses the words "south," "east," "wind," and "rain" in predictions—slurring the words together to form one word: "southeastwindrain." After a week of beautiful and amazing sunny weather, we are back to the normal southeastwindrain forecasted far into the immediate future. A new word for the Alaskan language might be "northwestwindsun," but it wouldn't be used very often.

Journal Entry #24
Crabbers Symphony
June 19 & 20, 2006
Exchange Cove Alaska

After spending the night at St John's Harbor on Zarembo Island, and catching a small halibut for dinner, we motored to Exchange Cove, continuing our southbound journey against the wind. We trolled our squids and flashers as we went, trying to keep our cost per fish caught at a level above the grocery store. Combined, our licenses in Alaska added up to $325.00 for the season and we had about ten pounds of fish so far, most of it consumed. This did not include the money spent on fishing gear, which amounted to a nice additional sum. I'd say we were at $50 per pound.

As we fished, we also "spied" using binoculars to see what others were doing or catching and, in addition to using binoculars, it was also entertaining to eavesdrop on the VHF radio and listen to boaters' conversations. There were warnings not to run over gill nets; discussions of the crab catch; salmon catch; what crew members were on board; comments as to their seaworthy abilities; a comparison of the weather from last year and this year (both terrible); rough crossings; who bought what boat; where and how much; what licenses came with the boat; engine breakdown reports; and commiserations, etc. The VHF conversations really give you a glimpse of the commercial fisherman's life.

We fished quite a bit in the murky waters of the Stikine River area with no results, but we hoped in less silt-filled waters the salmon just might see the flashers that Captain Bob kept polishing so diligently. The water got clearer the further south we got, and slack came and went and still no salmon. We were ready to quit and anchor for the night when a lone eagle came streaking past the Shadowfax with his legs extended for a catch. He hovered a few feet off the water with talons extended, paused, circled, and flew back having missed his chance. We took advantage of our own personal "spotter" and trolled through the area and caught two salmon, a nice sockeye and a king. If we could have figured out which eagle was our spotter, we would have gladly given him a share.

We anchored again in an Alaskan crab pot minefield and were entertained by the crabbers as they entered the bay and hauled in their pots. It was not a silent harvest—the diesel engine vibrato, the staccato whacks as the crab bait is cut up for the pots, and the tympanic thumps as the pots are thrown back have a certain tune and rhythm: The Crabbers Symphony.

Journal Entry #25
Bounced and Trounced
June 21, 2006
Coffman Cove Prince of Wales Island, Alaska

Today was not one of our better sailing days. As soon as the small craft warnings in Clarence Strait were downgraded and the wind appeared to be getting weaker, we headed south to Thorne Bay—a short 25 miles down the coast. What a learning experience we had. The Alaskan forecasters mean 20 *Alaskan* knot winds. Captain Bob figured it was blowing at least 25 *Washington* knot winds.

We were doing fine with a reefed jenny (no main) on a port tack doing six to seven knots until the wind freshened and we had six to eight foot seas on the nose and the tide against us. Suddenly the six to seven knot speed dropped down to one knot and we switched on the engine for added power. We were close to a threatening rocky shore with no lee, lots of reefs (visible because of the crashing surf) and the current pushing us towards them. At this point, none of the harbors in front of us seemed to be attainable goals, so we aborted our course and returned to Coffman Cove. Basically we sailed clear across Clarence Strait and back again—a total of 12 long nautical miles. The rougher the water, the longer the nautical miles become, which is something known as "Watt's Law."

When we got back to the dock and gladly slunk back into our old space from the past night, we spoke to some people and found out that they considered this to be windy weather so we didn't feel so bad about making the decision to turn back. Turns out we had gotten within two nautical miles of our goal, and we couldn't make it, but we had a good sail.

The community of Coffman Cove, the Alaskan government, and the U.S. Forest Service were sponsoring an archeological dig on one of the many Indian middens in the area. There is the potential of digging through 8,000 years of layered history but not in the two week timeframe allotted to this particular dig. Since the volunteers were being housed in small tents in a mosquito bog, two weeks was probably as long as they could take. The muddy volunteers crouched in the rain and scraped what appeared to be blackened dirt, mud, and stones. They hosed off the scrapings and sifted these through wire mesh. A First Nation's monitor was reviewing any findings. The area chosen to excavate, in carefully blocked off squares, was an old logging camp staging area which had been bulldozed and contoured. It seemed an unlikely choice for a site.

There is the potential of blocking any further economic development in the area if enough significant historical remains are found, so I wondered if they really even wanted to find any artifacts.

Journal Entry #26
Synopsis
June 23, 2006
Thorne Bay, Alaska

The Shadowfax and its crew have finally figured out how the Alaskan schedule works. It has to do with daylight, weather, and wind. In response to the long daylight hours in the summer (3:30 A.M. to midnight), people have adjusted their schedules. If one needs to move around on the water, then wind and tides dictate the working hours, not a human schedule of nine to five. We left Coffman Cove early one morning after waking up at 3:30 A.M. to beat the wind and to take advantage of the tides. This allowed us to reach Thorne Bay by 2:00 P.M. with a minimum of thrashing by the waves.

Thorne Bay has the nicest docks in the area. Someone spent a lot of time writing grants to get the funds to put in the wonderful docks, nice garbage dumpsters, walkways, new gas dock, RV pump stations, and tourist guide books. At least at this time of year the area doesn't seem to have been discovered. There was plenty of dock space and absolutely no tourist trap stores, one grocery store, the obligatory liquor store, no laundry, and the only restaurant was a takeout stand in the process of being remodeled over a long period of time. There was a small convenience store/seaplane depot at the gas dock with a few sundries and snacks.

It was surprising to meet someone from our old neighborhood in Kirkland, Washington who attended the same schools as our own children. The couple lives and works in Thorne Bay, apparently studying the area's geology, doing some land use planning, and running the liquor store. An even greater coincidence is that the husband wrote his thesis about the geology of Waldron, Skipjack and Bare Island in the San Juan Islands near our own Stuart Island. At our expression of interest, we were invited inside to look at the thesis. Their cozy house was filled with rock collections, fossil collections, books, and animal head collections. They practically had a zoo hanging on the walls in the living room. An eerie feeling to look into all those expressionless and staring eyes.

We are certainly getting to know the idiosyncrasies of the Shadowfax. If the upper deck around the mast dries out, it will leak for a day until the rains make the area "take-up" as Captain Bob says. It'll probably be a winter repair project—hopefully not of major proportions. The diesel gas vent allows seawater intrusion into our fuel tanks as we motor sail when the port rail (where the vent is located) is immersed or splashed by salt water. The resultant water will clog the fuel filter and is not good for the engine, and creates another repair project. Counter intuitively, the switch on the inverter is always to be "off" since it is controlled by the Link 2000 module. The sink in the head will spew out water in large spurts onto the cabin floor while under sail on a port tack as waves slap the hull and water is forced up inside the drain.

The engine compartment was never designed to properly vent a hard working diesel, unless the service door is propped open so the engine doesn't get too hot. The diesel furnace (repaired this spring) is also air starved so we have learned to never cover or block the side where the air intake is or the sensor will trip the electrical fuse. The forward shower bilge pump only works when the water pressure switch is on. We tried to replace that pump until we figured out it just needed power. Ditto for the freshwater tank gauge. Captain Bob opened the tank and cleaned the sending unit before he realized that the vapor detector for the stove had to be on to power the gauge.

We decided to skip more sightseeing in the area and take advantage of the wind and tide to continue our voyage south. It was tempting to keep traveling and investigating more of the native sites and their abandoned totem poles, but it was time to head back. Hopefully to sunnier and warmer places!

Journal Entry #27
The Fishing Boat Gauntlet
June 24 & 25, 2006
Dixon Entrance AK & BC

Leaving Ketchikan's rain behind, we took advantage of some calm winds and headed south for Prince Rupert and British Columbia. The whole Alaskan gill net fleet must have accompanied us because we had quite a time dodging boats with their gill nets stretched out for hundreds of feet behind them. I counted fifteen different vessels around us most of the way past Foggy Bay and Tree Point. The swells from the open ocean are large enough so that there is no way to see the gill nets and their orange buoy markers. You would think that the buoys would be really large with highly visible flags to warn away vessels, but no such luck. It gets even more interesting when the fishermen leave their nets unattended with only the buoys on each end in wait for either fish or unwary boaters to get ensnared. They lurk off in the distance watching their nets.

We turned on our VHF radio to Channel 16—the emergency calling channel, but even when we headed right for a net there was no outraged warning squawk from its fishing boat. We zigged and zagged our way towards Prince Rupert heading for British Canadian customs. We will spend the night in U.S. waters and then cross in the morning, perhaps having an opportunity to lower the cost per pound of Alaskan fish by catching a halibut or salmon. We fished in our moorage last night and caught a dogfish big enough to break the fishing pole and steal the lure, so our cost per pound continues to rise. The moorage was not highly rated by our guide book, but we thought it was a great anchorage complete with bright yellow seaweed—the same shade as scotch broom, festooning the rocky beaches.

As we make our way into Nakat Bay for our last night in Alaskan waters, the Pacific Ocean waves are putting on quite a show on the rocky shore. Waves are exploding over shoals. Without a GPS, the rocks would be invisible as they are lying just below the surface until exposed by a receding swell and then covered again by the next incoming one. I wouldn't want to attempt entering this inlet in a storm. The cross on one point nearby illustrates what can happen to the unwary or unlucky.

Nakat Harbor was teaming with fish at all different depths according to our fish finder. The fish pictures filled the screen at 118 feet, 58 feet, 36 feet, and 25 feet. Our adrenaline was up, until we looked down into the water and saw the jellyfish. These generated the images that were showing up on our fishfinder! Hundreds of jellyfish of every possible color: scarlet, orange, lemon yellow, cream, brown, and many varying hues of white. They pulsed along beside the Shadowfax in grape to grapefruit sized spheres with impossibly long translucent tentacles in halos around them. We estimated one bunch of tentacle strands to be six feet long. This put an end to any ideas of fishing.

Shadowfax seems to have a "thing" with Prince Rupert. We made repairs on the way up, and now we need to make repairs on the way down. A whiff of hot oil smell got us on the alert, and sure enough we had an oil leak under the engine. It was a minor leak at the oil sending unit—an oozing seepage really, so we will have to add a quart and tighten some fittings. That's the optimistic point of view. In reality we will probably break off the fitting, and have to "easy out" the pipe and send it to Seattle for parts to be flown back on Kenmore Air which should take an extra week or two.

Journal Entry #28
Gremlins on Board
June 26, 2006
Nakat Harbor, Alaska

The Shadowfax has mysterious happenings that seem to be getting worse. The fresh water pump will start running for no reason, as if an invisible gremlin crew member had turned on a faucet. What started as a minor annoyance has now turned into a major problem and we are forced to turn off the pump at night or it will run, waking us and wasting our precious power. We have managed to deal with the pump gremlin, but it seems to have multiplied.

The inverter stopped providing 120 V cabin electrical power. We disassembled the fuse panel and found that the gremlins had untwisted some wires. Under engine power, the tachometer and charging system will stop and start functioning for no apparent reason—no loose wire, no disconnected gauge, nothing. The vapor detector will shriek at odd moments, although I suspect that Pam Spray, Nutra-air, or even garlic smells are the culprits, not gremlins.

Then there is the sourdough issue. No matter what kind of container this gooey batter is put in, it spills in the ice chest, in the sink, and on the counter—dribbling down the cabinet fronts and into the freezer. This sourdough was a precious acquisition in Ketchikan and must be saved, hoarded, cherished, and protected. The freezer spill was pretty nasty due to the fact that two containers of sourdough were created in separate places to outsmart the gremlins and ensure the dough's survival. The sourdough sloshed over the halibut and salmon fillets, coated the ice cubes, oozed over the frozen fish heads (for halibut bait), and pooled in the bottom of the freezer. Worse yet, we didn't discover the spill until it had become a congealed, frozen, impossible to clean-up mess. I wonder if Prince Rupert has exterminators.

Journal Entry #29
Watt Power = Horse Power
June 27, 2006
Prince Rupert, BC

The dire prediction of disaster regarding the engine repair has been partially fulfilled. The engine oil gauge fitting did break off, but only because it was already cracked. We were extremely lucky that the last day of running was by sail or we probably would have pumped all the oil out of the engine into the bilge!

Reaching Prince Rupert we were unable to find moorage, so we found a secure anchorage in a small cove nearby. We purchased parts in town and made satisfactory repairs. That's the good news. The bad news is it was a secure anchorage so the anchor wouldn't come up no matter what.

We tried pulling in every direction, circling the anchor, powering forward, reversing, but nary a budge from the anchor. Time to don the scuba apparel and check out the problem up close! So Captain Bob suited up and headed below. Bubbles of compressed air showed his route along the bottom. I could measure his activity level by the volume of the bubbles. The more effort underwater, the larger the air intake by the diver and the resultant expulsion of air causing the bubbles. Watching from above, it was obvious when he found the anchor and started hauling on it to free it, as air bubbles percolated up in a bubbling—boiling mass indicating his progress. The anchor line slacked and pulled as he worked below, freeing what turned out to be a total snarl of anchor and chain encircling an old metal boat hulk.

The Shadowfax swung and swayed from the pulling below and from the wind gusts above until the anchor was freed and the boat started sliding along with the wind. This was one event we had not foreseen and for a moment panic set in. Starting the motor wasn't an option with a diver below and I was hoping the diver would surface so we could make our next plan. Suddenly the Shadowfax, all 40 feet and 9 tons, started slowly moving forward against the wind and current. Captain Bob had grabbed the anchor underwater and was slowing swimming the boat forward to a clear anchorage.

ONE WATT POWER = ?? HORSE POWER

Journal Entry #30
Kxngeal and Txagiu
June 28-30, 2006

Leaving Prince Rupert, we headed south, opting for the outside route so as not to backtrack. Unfortunately the wind wasn't co-operating and we had to run the engine. The Shadowfax was not pleased, and after three hours, the voltage regulator failed (the second failure in a month). So, we anchored in a temporary harbor, replaced the regulator with our only spare and then headed down the more protected inner passages.

Gremlins were still at work and the tachometer and charging gauges showed that the voltage regulator was still not functioning correctly. The Shadowfax obviously wanted to sail, not run on the iron jenny (the sailor term for engine). There was some wind, and with the currents in our favor, we hoisted the jenny to travel down Grenville Channel. The "some" wind got stronger and soon we were traveling at speeds of seven and eight knots on only one sail. With the wind came three to four foot waves with whitecaps and our speeds crept up to nine knots. Were we in charge, or was the Shadowfax?

As we traveled faster and faster with the wind, we wondered if we should pull into a harbor while we were still in control and not the boat. We were familiar with Kxngeal Harbor, having anchored there on the way north, so we decided to hang a sharp left turn and enter the bay. We skidded around the point in a 180 degree turn doing seven or eight knots with the port rail in the water. For a few moments it felt as if the Shadowfax had taken control! Now we truly understand how well the Shadowfax is named. Horses are temperamental. They like to run, buck, gallop, take the bit in their teeth and generally be headstrong.

Anchoring in our previous site we watched the wind gusts get stronger, it blew 12-15 knots in our bay with gusts up to 20 knots. The outside channel must have been truly wicked at this point, so it was a good thing we stopped our headlong charge down the channel when we did.

The next morning, all was calm, so we headed out to catch the NW winds to take us to Txagiu, also known as Hartley Bay. We had hoped to find some way of obtaining spare repair parts, but no such luck. Txagiu is the home of the Gitga'at Nation, a tiny town with boardwalk streets for four wheelers, no real stores, free moorage, no dock power, and some fuel. Houses are neat, newer modern split levels built on timber supports over the rocky hillside; all connected by wooden stairs and boardwalk bridges. One boardwalk is a mile long, leading to the local lake, swimming hole, and huckleberry patches. It has been repaired and patched, but the open holes and broken boards attest to the potential to crash through the walkway at any time. There seems to be an on-going siding repair effort on the houses because of the dampness and mold. A number of the houses were in the process of being totally gutted and re-sided. Even the houses that had been done the year or two before already had black mold coating the exteriors and would probably need more repair.

An animal or bird pen was set up outside one house, puzzling due to the lack of inhabitants except for a large rubber owl. Perhaps not so puzzling since the haphazard arrangement of the netting enclosing the cage would make it impossible to contain any critter with such loose construction. Later, walking past the enclosure, the riddle was solved. It was not a pen to enclose. It was meant to protect the fresh salmon strips that were hung inside to dry in the sun. The owl was meant to frighten off marauding birds or crows.

The Gitga'a Nation is attempting to promote its culture, displaying a beautiful wooden cultural center and a fish hatchery. The fish hatchery seemed to be non-functional with empty hatchery tanks, and weeds covering the area. Either all the activity occurs in the fall, or all the nets lying on the boardwalks at the head of the salmon stream have ended the fishing runs and there are no more eggs to harvest.

We were told that two young men had been sent to study native woodcarving for a year at the University in Vancouver and had started a totem pole. Much like the fish hatchery, the totem pole work seemed to be on hold. The young men were out fishing and hadn't done much on the pole for quite a while.

Travels such as this with the Shadowfax are ripe for coincidences and connections with people and past events. At Hartley Bay, we met up with four fishermen who told a strange tale of a north coast caretaker. Seems the men were halibut fishing on an early snowy spring weekend when they tied up at the dock. Since it was bitterly cold and freezing the fisherman offered the caretaker a comradely drink of rum. The caretaker gleefully accepted the offer, took the rum bottle, downed most of it in one long drink, handed the remains back with a "Yee-haw!" and then promptly collapsed on the floor of the boat in a stupor. The fishermen decided to let the caretaker sleep it off where he lay since it was warm enough inside the boat cabin. They left one person to "guard" the caretaker while the other three were cleaning halibut. After a time the "guard" came running wild-eyed to the upper deck of the boat where the cleaning was taking place and shouted that the caretaker "Was in the drink!" The response from the fish cleaners was simple…

"Well, take the bottle away!"

"You don't understand…He's *in* the drink!"

The caretaker had fallen overboard and would have drowned if one of the fishermen hadn't noticed a lone hand forlornly resting on a nearby log. The hand was attached to the submerged semi-comatose caretaker who was hauled out to dry out for the night under a watchful guard on the fishing boat. Other reports from other sailors who encountered the caretaker after the submerging reported that there were no serious ill effects other than a light limp which the caretaker freely admitted was due to "getting into the juice."

The Gitga'at Nation cares for the dock and hot springs at Bishop Bay further to the north and east. The familiar wooden boardwalks with recent repairs similar to those in Hartley Bay attest to their vigilant attempts to preserve the environment. The clear water in the springs is piped to three enclosed pools—hot, not so hot, and warm. A welcoming bench, newly constructed, which provided for bathers comfort, by the Gitga'at was already displaying graffiti, including a note from Grand Bank's 2006 (the Pride). We didn't leave any messages.

We were waved over to the dock to raft up with the Lisa II owned by a couple named Mario and Rosa. They had their entire family including three year-old and five year-old grandchildren onboard, which made us feel very homesick. With similar ages and family structures, we hit it off and soon everyone was sharing Captain Bob's birthday pie and Mario's homemade grape wine.

Journal Entry #31
Of Snarling Seals and Swarming Horseflies
July 2-4, 2006
Khutze Inlet, Fraser Reach BC

The five mile inlet of Khutze Bay is surrounded by 4,000 foot mountains all pouring snow melt downward into the sound. Fan shaped sprays of gravel debris dotting the length of the bay attest to the force of the earlier snow melt. One such gravel fan was spewed with such vertical force down the mountain that a spit extending almost across the mouth of the bay has formed over time. Makes for good anchoring!

We decided to anchor in the farthest end of the bay near waterfalls, rivers, and a large muskeg delta. The spectacular waterfall we finally anchored near spilled from 2,500 feet above the Shadowfax. We could watch the white streaks of water shooting straight down, jumping from rocky outcropping to outcropping until vanishing from view at the base of the cliff in a tangle of boulders and trees.

The delta, made up from five rivers, spread out in front of us with a friendly invitation to explore, so we got the Shadow ready and headed up a tributary. Wow! We saw birds galore, a seal nursery, fledgling ducks, mergansers, even eagles nesting. For a moment, we thought we saw flying fish, and then remembered this was not the Caribbean or Palau in Micronesia. The small objects skipping across the surface of the bay were small swimming seabirds exuberantly erupting from the watery depths where they had been fishing.

We didn't see any bears or moose, but we soon discovered the reason for the absence—they would have been eaten alive. Hoards of biting horseflies were waiting to attack any living creature, including us. We motored gamely on however, swatting a swath in front of the dingy with an oar. The flies seem to have some intelligence. They hide until their victims have let their guard down, then attack in full force. The Shadow was finally routed by the flies and we made our escape (we thought) back to the Shadowfax and our mosquito netting, unneeded until now. The flies accompanied us back, following the dingy, even landing on the sides of the boat and holding on with feet and mandibles to obtain a free ride and conserve energy for a fresh onslaught.

As we made our escape back along the river, we got too close to one of the seal nurseries. An irritated mother seal, sensing our vulnerability, swam toward us growling to warn us to stay away from her baby. We took the hint.

Reaching the Shadowfax, we closed up the dodger area with all the mosquito netting available, but the horseflies crawled in every little opening and attacked. They infiltrated around zippers, snaps, fittings and hatches. We tried spraying them with bug spray, hanging fly paper, vacuuming, swatting them with hands, hats, and cooking spatulas, but the onslaught was overwhelming. They bit hunks of flesh from bare spots and even were able to stealthily land and nip through denim jeans. From a distance we probably appeared to be doing a German Shoeplattler Dance sans Lederhosen. We finally went to our last line of defense by encasing ourselves in the interior of the Shadowfax with two layers of mosquito netting and waited for the cooler evening temperatures to put a stop to the attack. We left first thing the next morning.

Journal Entry #32
The Salmon Head
July 5, 2006
Bolin Bay, Fjordland, BC

Halibut fishing success depends on two things: the proper bait and the availability of a halibut in the vicinity of that bait. The best bait according to the fishing guides in Sitka and in our own past experience are salmon heads. Salmon heads are to be treasured and saved, frozen in zip-lock bags for future use, displacing ice cream, meat, and other frozen goods in the freezer. They are even re-used by quickly encasing the heads in zip-lock bags and whipping them back into the freezer after abortive fishing attempts. These treasured fish tempters are fastened onto fishing poles with heavy test line, wire leader, large hooks, and one and a half foot long metal rods with a one pound round lead weight attached.

We lower this contraption 200-300 feet to hook the "big one." Because of the effort involved, we only use this masterpiece of fishing tackle in a spot we consider perfect for halibut. Bolin Bay was such a spot—deep water off the bay, shelving areas, sand areas and, most importantly, fish visible on our state-of-the-art Garmin fish-finder.

We loaded up the Shadow with our equipment and started the outboard, only to find that the small motor's water pump wasn't functioning, so it wouldn't run. So we rowed our little eight foot foldable dingy, Shadow, still hoping to land the big one. Captain Bob got the first fish with his light pole, a nice yellow eye, so we knew we were in the right depths, but nothing on the halibut pole, so we moved to a different spot. It turned out to be a good move.

First a nip on the halibut pole, then a bottom snag, and then an attempt to yank the tackle free, but the bottom took off. The Ugly Stick (a special halibut fishing pole we use) bent double under the dingy and the fish attempted to pull pole, tackle, and fisherwoman into the water. The drag was a teeny bit tight. When I loosened the drag, it didn't help because the line simply spooled off the reel. I even made a futile attempt to increase some drag by putting my thumb on the line and ended up with a burnt thumb.

At this point it occurred to me that this might be a problem. We had no motor, a small boat, and a fish capable of pulling the Shadow around the bay, so I gave the pole to Captain Bob to subdue our catch. We were no longer the hunters, we had become the prey. He only had the fish for a moment, when thankfully, the fish let go of us. We retrieved the bait and found out what saved us. The hooks on the bait head had been smashed into the head of the salmon, so as to inactivate the barbs.

Chastened, we took the yellow eye back to the boat for dinner and discarded the salmon head. I think I'll stick to the little white rubber worm for fishing bait in the future.

Journal Entry #33
Remnants of "The Pride"
July 6, 2006
Kynoch Inlet, Fiordland Recreational Area, BC

We keep running into the remnants of the Grand Banks 2006 boating group (The Pride) we first encountered in Shoal Bay on our way up to Alaska.

This group, complete with a continuous blog on the internet, traveled from Nanaimo BC to Wrangell Alaska to celebrate the 40 or 50 year anniversary of Grand Banks Yachts. We can see them coming from a distance, and can identify them by color, they are white, and by their order, they look like ducklings following a mother hen. They were on their way into Kynoch Inlet as we were battling our way out against wind and tide.

Kynoch had been our destination, but the eight and half mile long inlet provided a channel for the wind with a venturi effect so the anchorage at the end was too rough for the Shadowfax. We returned to Bolin Bay for a repeat calm anchorage there instead. If the Grand Banks blog is still operational, we may find out how their evening at the end of Kynoch went.

Kynoch Inlet is a BC Park in the Fiordland Recreational Area and no, a picture isn't worth a thousand words. You can't capture the scale of the area, even with digital camera or video. The mountains go straight up from the water and are so steep and rugged that few trees, ground cover, moss, or in many cases even soil can stick to the glacially carved features. Granite Grey is the major color with a few wisps of greenery where the mountains reach into the water.

One mountainous stone buttress resembled an unfinished Mount Rushmore, with solemn features and dark eye sockets facing towards the east. The heights of the peaks start at 3,500 feet and plunge down to 1,200 fathoms in the fjord-like waters. The shores of the inlet are steep enough to tie the boat against, much like the vertical walls of the Ballard locks in Seattle, with only the rise and fall of the tide to prevent satisfactory moorage. Waterfalls pour straight down cliffs, in some cases shooting out with such force that the water travels twenty-five feet horizontally before continuing the downward plunge. We were fortunate to have clear skies and sunshine to enjoy this spectacular scenery.

Journal Entry #34
To Reef or Not to Reef, That Is the Question
July 7, 2006
Bella Bella/Shearwater, BC

The training regime of the Shadowfax has been working well. We now sail every chance we get since traveling at 1,200 rpm will barely get us moving, whereas a main plus jenny can generate seven to eight knots, depending on available wind. We have not destroyed our last voltage regulator yet by means of the reduction in engine rpm and resultant reduction of the high charging rate of the super alternator. To further insure longevity of the voltage regulator, we have taken steps to keep the engine compartment super cool. This involves opening all access hatches around the engine, running a blower, and keeping cabin portholes opened up. Our bunk lies next to the engine, so you can imagine how hot our sleeping berth gets. Our vigilance includes checking the engine gauges every few minutes to see if we have blown up our last voltage regulator.

With all this sailing, I have come to realize that it is OK to use that dreaded four letter word "reef." It just means to take in a sail in case of heavy winds. Both our main sail and our jenny can be reefed, and the Shadowfax seems to like sailing better with something reefed if the winds hit twenty. I am sure Captain Bob has a different opinion of this reefing business. I know I am a chicken, but I like sailing with a feeling of control of the boat, not having the boat control me.

Poor little Shadow is being towed along behind the Shadowfax, tethered on a yellow poly line, swinging from side to side and sometimes sliding and bumping into the stern of the bigger vessel when waves get too big. Last year the Shadow made one abortive attempt at escape but was quickly recaptured. This year the dingy is apparently resigned to its fate, although I did notice that it tried to guide our evening row back, not to the Shadowfax, but back to a neighboring boat with a dingy davit. Obviously poor Shadow wants to ride in splendor hanging off the stern attached to a davit, not be dragged ingloriously behind. The boat is designed to fold up and fit on deck, but it is a tedious job to take apart and put together, so we have found it more convenient to tow—unfortunately for Shadow.

Today's tow for the dingy took 13 hours and we traveled 50 miles with the wind and tide against us, but the weather was getting questionable and we wanted to get to a secure harbor. It's a good thing we did because they are calling for storm warnings with high winds. We have ended up at Shearwater Resort at Bella Bella, unfortunately anchored out in an exposed position because all the docks are full.

At the last moment before the storm hit, the harbormaster took pity on us and allowed us to tie to the dock, thankfully in a coveted inside position. We doubled up our mooring lines, hooked up to the dock's electricity, and prepared to wait out the storm in comfort.

It is midnight and the winds are starting…

Journal Entry #35
Storm Force Winds
July 9, 2006
Bella Bella/ Shearwater

We spent two nights securely moored at the Shearwater Marina docks before the storm finally blew itself out. Winds at the docks were clocked at 39 knots, which was much better than the 50 knots predicted. The Shadowfax spent the worst windy night loudly singing to herself and creaking in the wind gusts. The bumpers squeaked, the rigging whistled, the waves smacked the sides and the hull flexed and heaved up and down. The wind sounded like a group of medieval monks crooning, accompanied by howling crescendos as the gusts peaked. According to the weather forecasters this was an unexpectedly intense low for this time of year.

In the aftermath we heard two requests from the coast guard for information on missing vessels. One such boat was a rowing kayak whose owners we may have met at Lagoon Cove and again at Prince Rupert. The rowers/kayakers were a father-son team in a specially designed craft trying to row from Prince Rupert to Sitka. The support "team" was the wife and mother who traveled solo up the coast a few days ahead of them in a 40 foot trawler. We will probably never hear what happened to the rowers.

We were able to hop a water taxi to Bella Bella when the winds subsided to look over the native settlement and its totem poles. There wasn't a lot to see, just the typical split level wood sided houses with peeling paint whose yards consisted of thimbleberries, weeds, long grass, and abandoned boats. Some of the houses were seemingly deserted with moss covered roofs, broken windows, and moldy paint, but the well worn pathways to the dilapidated, albeit functional, front stairs spoke a different story about the status of habitation. Other houses had been abandoned and left to return to nature, with collapsed roofs and missing walls. This is evidently in keeping with the old ways, the only trouble being that modern materials don't decompose like the older traditional building materials did. Rare behavior compared to treatment of the suburbs where we live, but it seems to be the accepted fashion here.

Then there are the dogs: dogs of every shape, tail length, curl, color, and size—no two alike in any way. Dogs with hairy ears, dogs with hairy feet, big ones, little ones and all were friendly, much too friendly. They came up for petting, they leaned on our legs. Soon they were jumping up for closer attention, licking, panting, drooling and even grabbing our coats in an attempt to get us to take them home. None growled or barked. Intimidating behavior, but delivered with such happy enthusiasm on the dog's part, not a scary experience for us.

Town residents were well-groomed, well-fed, happy and equally friendly with welcome smiles for wandering strangers. We were even informed we should attend a local wedding that was taking place later in the afternoon. Eating a late lunch in the one local cafe/pseudo 7- Eleven store, we found out the reason for the rounded waistlines: deep fat fried chicken, french fries, shrimp, halibut. You name it, I think they fried it. Our last purchase before we climbed on the water taxi for our trip back to Shearwater was Extra-Extra Strong 750 mg Tums.

Journal Entry #36
Howling Pack of Whales
July 10, 2006
Hakai Pass, BC

We left Shearwater and Bella Bella when the winds had subsided and headed down Lama Passage and Fitzshugh Sound. Fortunately the wind and tides were with us and we managed to find enough wind to sail. We headed silently southwards down the channel with mainsail and jenny for our destination of Goldstream Harbor, near Hakai Pass.

Nearing the end of the sail, our passage became not so silent with strange noises emanating from the rigging. The noise was a grating growling sound, low pitched and consistent. My insides knotted up from anxiety. Looking out toward the stays, blocks, and halyards on the front deck, I tried unsuccessfully to pin-point the source. This went on for quite a while with my stomach feeling sicker and sicker until I realized the noise was coming from a beach a mile and a half away from us—not from the Shadowfax.

A pod of killer whales had closed in for the kill and were having a great time chasing their fishy prey. Using binoculars we counted six whales breathing in unison, spewing white breathy fountains of steam, eight to ten feet in the air. They jumped, dove, slashed, swirled, thrashed, and splashed and as they did so they howled. It was a guttural raspy noise, almost a honk that carried well over the water.

Leaving the killer whales behind, we started an approach to Goldstream Harbor only to encounter another kind of whale, a lone pilot whale. This was a shy whale, no shouting for it, but it too had steamy breath. Unfortunately, we got too close so we were treated to a dose of "whale breath." It reminded me of what an outhouse might smell like if a family of minks built a nest inside and stored their cache of rotten fish carcasses there. Another tummy troubling moment!

We had an uneventful, non-windy night in Goldstream Harbor and in the morning proceeded down the channel towards Cape Caution only to encounter yet another kind of whale—humpbacks. These guys were lunging up from the depths to strain food through their huge mouths and throats. Very impressive to see the front half of a huge whale rise slowly straight up in the air and then subside again. Thankfully they were downwind.

Journal Entry #37
Ten Foot Seas and 25 Knot Winds
July 13, 2006
Jones Cove—Five Miles North of Cape Caution

We are hunkered down in a tiny cove waiting for the weather to calm down in Queen Charlotte Sound and Strait. I mention both, because it is difficult for me to define the exact place one ends and the other starts.

Our attempt to traverse Cape Caution today was defeated by the weather and our questionable engine. The Shadowfax was traveling at four to five knots with a reefed jenny and an engine running at a low rpm. With the wind and waves building, we decided to head for one of the few bays available in this rugged area, and by then we were only making two knots against the wind, waves, and currents. We couldn't see the entrance to Jones Cove's as we approached, only large white exploding waves with white foam swirling around the many nasty shoals in the area.

As we reached the cove, we could barely distinguish it from the surrounding cliffs, the entry point was so minuscule. We had one chance to surf our way into the small entrance, or the poor Shadowfax most likely would have ended up on the rocks. It was like threading a needle. Thankfully we made it.

The tide was low when we entered the tiny cove and we anchored as best we could with the bow of the Shadowfax projecting out into the surf. The cove was shallow, leaving five feet of water under our seven foot keel. In most conditions this would have been adequate but it was marginal, given the size of the swells that ricocheted from rock to rock around us. As the tide rose during the evening our protection from the surf grew even less as the rocky reef in front of the cove slowly submerged. We spent a sleepless night rocking and rolling in the surf that surged into the bay until dawn and calmer waters prevailed.

These storms are all called "unusually intense lows" by the weather forecasters on the VHF radio. Since we have had at least three or four of these lately, I don't understand what is unusual about them. They sit threateningly out in the Pacific, intensify, don't move as the forecaster's predict, and then suddenly spring onto the coast with the trough and associated front. The marine weather guru's scramble and quickly revise forecasts to reflect what is actually occurring and pretend they had it right all along. There should be a disclaimer prior to the broadcast, however it would take too long and the static would wipe out any useful information.

The Shadowfax handles weather better than I do with my artificial hips. I find the best position for me when the boat is in large waves is reclining in the salon, looking up, and watching the waves break over the bow of the boat and wash over the windows. The window leaks don't get any worse with a foot of water pouring over the cracks than they do in a steady rain. I envision the curved top deck of the Shadowfax as just being like a curved windsurfer, capable of withstanding quite an onslaught of sea water. Every now and then I climb above, hanging on like a monkey, to handle the helm while Captain Bob sees to the sails. Tums and Imodium IB help my stomach somewhat in such instances.

Jones Cove was certainly not as secure as our past anchorage in Frypan Bay for the last three nights. Frypan Bay was so enclosed that we could not tell what the weather was actually doing and we made a false start the day before in an attempt to move south. It was calm in the bay with no apparent wind, so we hoisted anchor and started out the protected entrance. We didn't get far when we realized our error and did an abrupt about-face back to the safety of Frypan Bay.

My joke as we first anchored there was that it would be the perfect place to be holed up waiting for calmer weather if only you could catch fish right off the boat. I should have added one more caveat—big enough fish to keep! We made four casts and caught four small rockfish—only big enough if you were truly starving. We threw them back and then ventured out in the Shadow to attempt to fish outside the bay in Darby Channel, but still caught only tiny rockfish, which we released.

One little fish appeared to be done for after hooking him at one hundred feet below and bringing him to the surface. He flailed along on the surface and we were in the process of netting him when we realized we had an audience. Three eagles were perched close to the Shadow on nearby trees and as the rockfish drifted tantalizingly close, the birds made a number of attempts to snatch the fish, but we were too near and frightened these birdie scavengers. One eagle would soar, put out its talons, lower for the pick-up, and at the last minute abort the operation.

The three eagles in the trees got closer and closer until the hungriest eagle couldn't stand it any more and finally took flight and successfully retrieved the fish. It proved to be our entertainment for the afternoon.

Journal Entry #38
The Glass Beaches of Mamalilaculla
July 16, 2006
Village Island, The Broughtons

The beaches of the abandoned Indian settlement of Mamalilaculla are bright—blinding white and sparkling in whatever sun is available. Well worn pieces of discarded items lie shimmering on the beaches: depression glass, beer bottles, medicine bottles, thick pottery, pieces of an old lace up boot, patterned chips of china, and more hauntingly, the tiny front half of a child's leather shoe.

The remnants of "clam gardens" can still be seen in the tidal areas of coves on Village Island, attesting to the importance of these bivalves in the native diet. Rocks were carefully piled along low tide marks of beaches, creating a rock fence—not to corral the clams, but perhaps to allow an easier harvest, indicate boundary lines, or provide the clam beds some protection from wave action during low tides.

Perhaps the gardens were considered private property and zealously guarded by the native farmers. Maybe giving rise to battles that rightly might have been called Clam Wars.

Old engine parts and hunks of metal, including enamel washing machine drums, reside rusting away in the tidal flats. It almost appeared from the placement of the debris that some of it may have been used for the utilitarian purpose of clam roasting, a fitting final end for the white man's tools.

This area, according to our guide book was continuously inhabited for 8,000 years by the native Indians and thrived until the 1920's. The fish disappeared and the old settlement was gradually abandoned, leaving the relatively "modern" wooden buildings with their associated docks to sprawl and decay alongside the more traditional remains of longhouses and totem poles. The site has reverted back to blackberries, thimbleberries, wild honeysuckle, humming birds, and bees. It is still an Indian Reserve, but we saw no evidence of recent habitation—just the ruins, shell middens, silence, and a number of grave sites dotting the islands surrounding Mamalilaculla.

The guide book urged us not to desecrate these sites with their large cement chests of human remains. Of course, we didn't.

Journal Entry #39
Shadowfax Takes Control
July 18, 2006
Whirlpool, Dent and Yaculta Rapids, Desolation Sound

Have you ever had a day when nothing went right? If anything could go wrong it did? Well the Shadowfax had such a day today. Well, maybe it was Captain Bob.

We had anticipated an ambitious day of travel to reach the warm and calm waters of Desolation Sound. There were three sets of nasty rapids to clear with different slack water times. We thought that a low powered boat like a sailboat (and particularly the Shadowfax with limited engine rpm) should only enter these dangerous tidal areas when the water wasn't traveling very fast.

We had three sources for current information and all three seemed to conflict—tide table books, the internet, and our Garmin computer. Needless to say, first thing in the morning it became apparent that we had not done our calculations properly and had set ourselves up for a whole day of travel against the current with little wind. We faced a grueling day unless we could squeeze every bit of energy from the almost non-existent wind. We were up for the challenge and decided to go downwind "wing-on-wing" with main. The jenny was held out by a huge spinnaker pole doing double duty as an improvised whisker pole. The pole was much too big and not ideal, but it was all we had and better yet, it worked.

In the excitement of installing the oversized pole on the bow of the Shadowfax, Captain Bob forgot to wear his life vest. A big no-no, one of our rules is that a life vest must be worn at all times when out of the cockpit. To facilitate this, we purchased some very high tech, streamlined, self-inflating and expensive life vests. Captain Bob, realizing his error, ran back and grabbed a vest, put it on, headed back out on the bow, snagged the activator pull, and ended up with a fully inflated life vest. He could barely move his head or arms, which isn't ideal for trying to sail the Shadowfax.

We decided this was not the end of the world and continued on, still with very little wind and against the current. We were going so slowly that it seemed to make sense to troll for some fish, since this area is prime salmon fishing grounds. Unfortunately, sailing, fishing poles, lures, sheets, and halyards make for a hazardous mix, and the hooks on the fishing lure got tangled in the jib sheet. Putting the Shadowfax on automatic pilot, Captain Bob once more got out on the bow to disengage the hooks. He did so, but managed to cut himself, so it was blood and band-aid time. As he was fighting the fishing poles, halyards, and hooks, the Shadowfax decided enough was enough and sent her boom across in a quick jibe to give the captain a smack on the side of his head. Not with enough force to do serious injury, just with enough force to get his attention.

So much for sailing on automatic pilot when the wind shifts!

Journal Entry #40
Bowling Ball Bay
July 19, 2006
Waddington Channel, Desolation Sound

As we have traveled south into Desolation Sound, we are revisiting areas that we spent time in over ten years ago, and what a change we are seeing. Older resorts are for sale or closing, the dwindling of the salmon runs and associated tourist trade are making it difficult to remain profitable. Minstrel Island Resort and Big Bay Resort are closed and sold. And Echo Bay is on the market with no takers.

To make a living, people in these areas are turning to aqua culture: fish farming, mussel farming, and oyster farming. Bays that once were pristine and beautiful anchorages are now filled with buoys, floats, rafts, machinery, and other unrecognizable, to us, tools of the aquaculture trade. Coves are roped off, and boaters have restricted access to the once public areas.

One such cove is near Allies Island. The sprawling oyster farm there is slowly and inexorably taking over the whole bay until the only available area for boaters is a narrow, straight fairway between a green buoy and a red buoy. The rest of the bay is literally covered with hundreds of black floats the size and shape of bowling balls. They bob in uniform patterns, lining up in apparent order, laid out with some undecipherable master plan. The floats are lightweight and float, but they resemble their heavier counterparts so closely that it is unnerving to see them lying on the surface of the water.

We watched power and sailboats slowly cruising past the labyrinth created by the floats, apparently trying to gain entrance, or perhaps just looking out of curiosity as to what these objects were. The whole oyster farm operation seems precarious, and we saw one black bowling ball float along with a larger blue barrel float make their escape from the area. We had thought the farm was unattended, but we did notice one lone skiff head for the dock and tie up. Soon we heard the echoing sound of a generator, and we perceived the farm was not as abandoned as it appeared at first glance. Evidently oysters don't require as much attention or care as much as the fish in the fish farms.

The Beekeeper of Refuge Cove, BC
July 24, 2006
Refuge Cove, Desolation Sound

Refuge Cove offers boaters one of the few places in Desolation Sound to obtain fuel, do laundry, take showers, buy supplies, groceries, books, magazines, hamburgers, ice cream cones, and even lattes. Wooden floats and docks provide tie-up areas from which deprived boaters can launch an attack on all the amenities available.

The small grocery store is divided into areas. One wall is dedicated to fishing tackle, camping necessities, house wares, and the boater's favorite assortment of epoxy, duct tape, and improbable miracle repair glues. Another part of the store is dedicated to books and magazines, which is important in this climate of either hot sun or incessant rain. The farthest corner has the obligatory small liquor store and just in case the alcoholic beverages are not enough of an enticement for customers, there is an ice cream freezer offering different varieties of ice creams. An adequate assortment of groceries and sundries are provided as a further draw, so customers can shop while doing laundry behind the back of the building where all the washing facilities are housed. Even free Wi-Fi internet access is offered from the docks. All in all, very respectable for this far out from civilization.

Located conveniently next to the laundry area is a small open air bookstore, providing comfortable reading benches and inviting shaded areas to sit and read. The owner dispenses philosophy along with the books he sells. Books are sorted by topic and prices with the apparent intent of guiding prospective customers into specific reading choices. He also sells home-grown honey if the reading matter isn't enough to sweeten one's day. The hives sit above the harbor in view of the bookstore so he can keep track of both of his products at the same time.

Children's books are the bargain of the day with four to five shelves devoted to paperbacks that cost 50 cents apiece—all quality reading material for ages five through fourteen. The acquisition of this treasure trove of books must have been planned and laboriously executed. The bookseller explained the literary treasure trove to me as I purchased some of these books for my grandchildren. "Children don't know how to read any more, I don't know what we are going to do when these kids grow up and all they do is watch computers or TV."

Sharing this reasonably priced book collection was perhaps his way of ensuring that reading as a skill would continue in the younger generation.

Journal Entry #42
The Shadowfax Strikes Again
July 25-27, 2006

Calm Channel, Teakerne, Squirrel Cove, Desolation Sound

What a prima donna the Shadowfax is turning out to be! When last we combined fishing with sailing, she clonked Captain Bob on the noggin with her boom, now it is fishing and motoring. The Shadowfax must be a tree-hugging, whale-loving, non-fishing environmentalist. We had slowed down to do some fishing in Calm Channel and were successful in landing two fish, when we noticed that the Shadowfax had sabotaged the voltage regulator again. No more charging from our alternator. What she doesn't know is that our boating friends are more than willing to let us hook up to their generators to charge our batteries while at anchor, and additionally we had stocked up on two more voltage regulators, in preparation for the inevitable regulator failures.

This attitude has got to stop, there is no such thing as non-fishing Watt boats. Of course we have never had a boat with an attitude before and we forgot the cardinal rule—never embarrass Shadowfax by hanging weird stuff off the stern. Last year she dumped off a very expensive pressure cooker from its perch on the barbecue. This year it was the plaid blanket draped on the back of the bimini to block the hot sun. I guess the plaid with its tasseled fringe was too much; it went over the side, down into Davy Jones Locker and stayed there despite Captain Bob's valiant attempts to dredge for it with hook, line, and buzz-bombs.

We have spent the past week with three power boats that belong to our long time friends, and poor Shadowfax has had to get used to rafting up in our moorages, the lone sailboat in our group. We are always the last to arrive at the chosen harbor for the evening due to our slower speed. The high boating season is here and there are many more boats in these harbors than when we were here in May. We counted 37 various cruising vessels in just one cove at Priedeux Haven, and 56 in the largest part of the harbor at Squirrel Cove. Sailboats appear to make up a respectable portion of the boats, probably due to the high fuel prices.

The Klahoose Indian Nation has a large sign on the shore at Squirrel Cove and the small town near the government dock has the appearance of possibly being connected to the First Nations, but the heritage is not as clear as the towns further north with their middens, prominent signs, artwork, and totem poles. A "Clahoose Village" at the end of Toba Inlet was mentioned in a history book—the notation dating back to 1888, so the pronunciation is good, but the spelling may be questionable.

The bay at Squirrel Cove is unique in that it houses a floating bakery, a log supported cheerful blue painted shed with signs proclaiming pies, cinnamon rolls, bread of all kinds, and other delicacies to be ordered in advance only. Our friends ordered cinnamon rolls for the next morning, and mentioned that the baker (a woman) was crabby, which isn't surprising given the high temperatures of the past week, and the fact that she apparently lives and (perhaps) cooks on the old wood tug boat moored next to the shed. Various informative signs adorned the wood float supporting the shed, stating hours, specific rules, trespass information, and even a can with a slot for orders and/or money to be deposited. I doubt anyone in the area would be brave enough to steal her money.

Squirrel Cove also has a lagoon and associated tidal rapids that either rush into the lagoon to fill it up, or pour out to empty the basin. When in full flood or ebb, kayaks and small rowing dinghies may be either stuck inside or outside the lagoon until slack water occurs hours later. This provides a free carnival—like a ride down the rapids for both adults and children. People use inner tubes, life vests, and kayaks—anything that floats to aid in the race down the rapids. Then they faced the problem of hauling their gear out along the edges of the shore for another ride that goes all too quickly.

Attire is informal, from swimsuits to t-shirts and shorts. We even saw an English Bulldog with swimming goggles secured over his eyes. The dog was tethered inside a dingy and not allowed in the water because he didn't swim well. We didn't understand the reasoning behind the goggles, but he was cute with them on!

Journal Entry #43
A Curious Collection
July 29, 2006
Walsh Cove, Desolation Sound

During the Inside Passage travels of the Shadowfax this year, I have purchased local cookbooks to add to my collection. Each little community has their own treasure trove of recipes that hint at the ethnicity of the area. Sizes range from 95 pages to 216 pages with the smallest harbor town of Coffman Cove, Alaska, spawning the largest cookbook and the most recipes.

Petersburg, Alaska recipes were definitely Scandinavian with Sylte Flesk, Rommegrot, Riskrem, Rulle-Polse, Sprutbakkelse and Headcheese—all details spelled out in the *Sons of Norway Fedrelandet Lodge 23 Cookbook.*

Most of the cookbooks feature a myriad of ways to prepare fish and shellfish bounty of the Inside Passage, although some are out of date. They feature recipes for items no longer available, or legal to harvest, such as abalone. Of course, the Alaskan cookbooks sometimes feature exotic items such as caribou, moose, elk, bear tenderloins, venison, chichee yitsee (seagull eggs) sourdough, rose hip catsup, Eskimo ice cream (using seal oil and reindeer fat), Seal's Bare Feet (Seal Flippers), Walrus Stew, and Keemuk (whale blubber). This, accompanied with a touch of Russian heritage, showcased by recipes of Kulich (Easter Cake), Russian tea, and Russian black bread makes for a truly eclectic recipe assortment.

The *Cortez Island Cookbook,* published in 1989 by the Cortez Island Seniors Building Society, is an interesting anomaly. I was curious as to how Eccles cake, pea oaties, pikelets, Scottish oatcakes, and bannock and porridge bread worked their way into its pages, providing competition for the fish and shellfish dishes. Turns out that a Scot, Michael Manson, started a trading post in 1882 at a place on Cortes Island and named it Manson's Landing. The Scottish influence reached further north in the naming of Bute Inlet, after either Bute County, Scotland with its "Kyles of Bute" or the House of Bute. Arran Rapids also shows Scottish influence—perhaps named for Arran Island in Scotland.

A fascinating note in my history exploration was that Marina Island was allegedly named for Hernadez Cortez's mistress, the fair Marina. Turns out he captured a group of unfortunate people during his privateering and she was among them. He made her his mistress and obviously, being very intelligent as well as beautiful, she cultivated his esteem. She made the best of what probably was an awful situation, and convinced him she was devoted and loyal. I wonder what the real truth was. I sense a good plot for a historical novel.

Journal Entry #44
Voltage Regulator Virus
July 30, 2006
Atwood Bay, Homfrey Channel, Desolation Sound

The Shadowfax destroyed our last transistorized voltage regulator and we have installed one of our two last voltage regulators. These regulators are antiques. They are mechanical and we purchased them from the auto parts store in Prince Rupert. Hopefully they will last longer than the previous two modern style regulators—each apparently destroyed by the inconsistent charging of the engine's alternator.

These mechanical regulators may outwit the Shadowfax's obvious desire to sabotage our charging, therefore our ability to run on the Westerbeke engine. We now watch the charging system like a hawk—waiting for one of three things to happen: overcharging at too high a voltage, undercharging at too low a voltage, or just not charging at all when both tachometer and charging system show zeros.

The newly replaced regulator's charging slowly creeps up 12.40, 12.60, 13.00, 13.55, 14.00, and up to 14.70 volts. Then when it hits 14.75, the charging is abruptly lowered to 13.50 before starting slow creep upward again. We feel like we are watching TV reruns on a 1 X 1 ½ inch screen. At least this regulator is behaving as it ought and shutting down when the charge gets too high.

The hope is that the proper voltage regulator will stop this non-charging cycle of events. The part has been specially ordered, probably especially expensive, and is to be available in three weeks. The automotive mechanical regulators were $10.00 each. The two prior failed transistorized regulators were $13.55 each (also automotive). And I bet this new regulator will be anywhere from $100 to $300 because it is marine. We will see.

Update: August, Refuge Cove, BC

We finally had the proper regulator flown in on a seaplane from Seattle. The shiny blue metal apparatus with a wiring harness cost $542.00. My estimate turned out to be a little low, but the added expense was worth it because it does seem to have handled our charging problem. The voltage regulator should have been replaced at the same time the faulty alternator was replaced last year. I guess the warranty didn't extend to matching the new alternator to a new voltage regulator. Replacing it at that time sure would have saved us a lot of time, effort, and trouble though.

Journal Entry #45
The Green Meditation Chair of Galley Bay
August 1, 2006
Galley Bay, Desolation Sound

The purpose of the east facing chair at the edge of the shoreline became apparent the morning after we anchored in Galley Bay. A bare-chested (possibly bare-everything) tanned young man came out from his cabin and sat facing the east. Sitting motionless in what I assume was the lotus position; he meditated in the warmth of the morning sun.

We had deliberately chosen Galley Bay for our harbor in order to see if there were any remains of an old commune left there. Part of the bay is in Desolation Sound Marine Park, and part of the bay is still in private, possibly communal hands. The original commune was started by a Gladys Nightingale (who changed her name to Sherrie Farrell) to support an on-going relationship with a free-spirited man named George Dibbern. This must have been in the 1940's. She allegedly shared him with a couple of other ladies, including his wife. (This is my extrapolation from the book *Dark Sun* by Erika Grundmann.)

Two hundred acres were purchased for this commune, and it was in use into the 1970's, at one time housing 100 members. I found a blog about the commune that described the nudity, pot, sexual activities, goat herding, gardening etc. It sounds like many of the more remote communes of that era minus the Bagwan.*

These hippies made quite an impression on the folks in the community at Lund according to the blogger. Perhaps because of some of the more outlandish activities practiced there, such as sending nude female swimmers out to accost passing boaters and beg for cigarettes.

We cruised around Galley Bay in the Shadow and were unable to pinpoint the exact place where the commune had been located. There were two obvious sites, one to the east and one to the west. The western site housed our meditator and looked the most "hippy-like" with some small cabins, some habitable, others not, some old fruit trees, rustic hot tubs, a rickety dock and many tiny sheds (some occupied) scattered around in the bushes and trees. One building was partially framed and perched out over the water on the hillside—roofless with missing walls and weathered siding. It appeared to have been abandoned in mid-construction. The site to the east had larger, less rustic homes and docks, but did have one older structure, which may have been the original home-site dating back to the 1940's. It had the appropriate appearance of the building described as the main structure by the blogger.

* http://boppin.com/ignoramus/2005/11/north.html

Journal Entry #46
Shadowfax and Shadow Succor a Seal Pup
August 2, 2006
Tenedos Bay, Desolation Sound

We anchored in the northwest end of Tenedos Bay near some small islets, a protective cove. We spent a quiet afternoon swimming in Unwin Lake and walking the trails through the old growth forest of the park. We arrived back at the Shadowfax and were in the middle of relaxing in the aftermath of another curry dinner when we noticed an odd brownish-grey log floating by the stern of the Shadowfax. It was shiny and smooth—maybe 18 inches long, had whiskers and was also breathing. It turned out to be the tiniest seal pup we had ever seen. As it floated, it slept, automatically exhaling underwater and rising for its next breath. We could be forgiven for not immediately recognizing that the "log" was alive, since the breaths were spaced out over a long period of time and our little seal pup was utterly motionless except for that gentle bubbling breath. What a darling creature!

We stewed over what to do for the little fellow, but remembered that the best rule in this situation, according to SPCA and Fisheries Management is to leave the pups alone. The mother seal will leave the pup for a time to forage for food and usually returns to retrieve the "abandoned" youngster. This pup was not malnourished. In fact he was a roly-poly grey ball—so rotund that his belly floated much higher than his head. Baby seal pups cry for their mothers both above the water and below the water where the sound carries 14 times further. Mother seals also can find their babies by acute sense of smell so we figured this pup was probably deliberately left in Tenedos Bay by its parent and she would be back. (This information was provided via a hasty search on the internet.)

We figured he would be ok if left alone, but the seal pup had other ideas. He was lonesome, not for human companionship, but for the companionship of other floating creatures—Shadow and Shadowfax. He stayed close all evening and into the night when he snuggled up between the hull of the Shadowfax and Shadow (right next to our sleeping area). We could hear his underwater exhalations and howls for Mom all night. I think the hull of the Shadowfax acted as an amplifier for his cries underwater, it certainly acted as an amplifier for us on the interior of the boat. In the morning he swam away, either finding his mother or his breakfast, and we hurriedly pulled anchor and took off.

Journal Entry #47
Fjord-Dwelling Golden King Crab
August 2, 2006
Atwood Bay, Desolation Sound

Would you believe we found king crab in the fjord-like inlets of British Columbia? It's true. One of the benefits as well as one of the problems of this instant broadband internet access during our travels is the ease of information collection. We've hatched all sorts of grand plans while surfing the net. As soon as we set up one plan, we get distracted by something else we want to find, and we come up with a different plan.

Homfray Channel is one of the deepest inlets around, and probably somewhere in its depth of 2,400 feet resides one of these crabs. One quick internet search tells me that a crab-sized pot, weighing 700 pounds and requiring a robust winch, would do the job if we ever located one of these critters. If putting out a shrimp pot with 400 feet of line is too much work for the crew of the Shadowfax, what about the king crab pot with nearly a half a mile worth of line? Then there is the loss factor. Shrimp pots get lost easily. Maybe we put the pots in water that is too deep for the length of the line we use, and maybe the currents are too strong, but at least we are only out about $150. If one of the king crab pots got away from us, it would be like letting a small car drift off, never to be seen again.

The educational and research value of the internet is incalculable. Crab info, First Nations info, commune dwelling, historical data, maps, pictures, area tips for exploring and anchoring—you name it and someone has a blog or website that contains the information you seek. When combined with books about the area, an internet investigator can be off on a fascinating quest.

Locating First Nations pictographs in Desolation Sound is an illustration of how this searching works. While reading a local book, *Waddington's Gold Road and the Bute Inlet Massacre,* I discovered that amongst the carnage and violence was a mention of pictographs in Homfray Channel. The location of the images was vague: "stand with Mount Addenbroke (and the pictographs) at your back and gaze across Homfray Channel towards Mount Denman." This would cover a lot of rocky coastline and be nearly impossible to locate, except for the additional information provided by the internet. Not only was the information available, there was even a map specifically detailing all the pictographs in the Desolation Sound area. Much more than the few sites mentioned in most guide books.

Another fascinating tidbit of information about the pictographs is how the red coloring was obtained. First Nation's people chewed red salmon eggs combined with burnt red oxide (red dirt), which when mixed with saliva, became a red paste-like paint that was used to create images on the rocky shorelines.

I bet modern graffiti problems would go away if the "artists" had to use salmon paste instead of store bought paint in spray cans.

Journal Entry #48
The One That Got Away...Again!
August 3, 2006
Atwood Bay, Desolation Sound

Four times in my fishing career I have had a fish so big on the line that the reel screamed, the drag was useless, the line reached its end and the lure snapped off: Minstral Island, fifteen years ago; Leask Lake area, ten years ago; Bolin Bay, and Atwood Bay, this year. The last two failures were due to a brain fade on my part. The idea of fishing is to land your catch—not to get something too big to successfully bring in. Big bait equals big fish, potentially too big.

Minstral Island and Leask Lake bait consisted of herring, the Bolin Bay lure was a salmon head—all natural baits, and they successfully attracted large fish. Atwood Bay was a Watt bait creation of mosquito netting, fresh fish pieces, and a lead head with a large red rubber worm attached. The mosquito netting contained the fish bait and was artistically crafted to resemble a white long legged octopus by strategic cutting of the netting. As a lure it looked superb, and the "octopus legs" fluttered convincingly in the salt water as the one foot in diameter lure rocked with the boat motion. I proudly lowered the lure into fifty-six feet of water, knowing that I would either get a big one or nothing at all—no mutilation of smaller fish. The ideal plan as a conservation measure.

The octopus lure worked. I had gone down below deck for a moment and that was all it took. The reel screamed, the line spooled out, and by the time I reached the pole all that was left was a few hundred yards of sixty pound test line pointing out in the direction the fish assailant had gone with the lure. The white line reached from our moorage out around the point (about 150 yards) and was forlornly floating on the surface without any lure or "octopus" attached.

Perhaps it was the sea serpent of Homfray Channel that figured in some First Nations stories. Fortunately, it got away!

Journal Entry #49
Mountain Goat Watt
August 3, 2006
Mt Whieldon , Atwood Bay, Desolation Sound

In Captain Bob's words, of his hiking and climbing experience at Atwood Bay here is the story:

The key to ascending Mt. Whielden is the dry creekbed. We returned to Atwood Bay the previous day. I started at 6:30 A.M. from the old log dump up the decommissioned logging road to find a climbing route to the summit of Mt. Whieldon. Views of the logged areas from Humphrey Channel made it appear that the abandoned logging roads reached nearly to the alpine areas of the mountain which would provide good access for ascending the peak.

I proceeded along the logging road for approximately two hours, at which time I arrived at the end of the primary haul road. The primary haul road is in excellent hiking condition and not overgrown with alder like most abandoned logging roads. I started along a secondary road which appeared to go in the direction I wanted. This road was being choked by alder growth, which made travel more difficult.

I arrived at a "Y" in the road and chose the lower because it appeared to be in better condition. After about fifteen minutes the alder became so thick it was impassible. I turned back discouraged. I decided to try the other road. After another fifteen minutes of swimming through the alder I was ready to quit again, then the alder thinned out for a while. The alder was buggy, sappy, and dirty.

I continued on for an hour in and out (mostly in) of the alder grove and then broke out of it. I spent the next half hour traversing piles of slash that had been dozed onto the road upon completion of the logging operations. The piles of slash were about ten feet high, thirty feet wide, and one hundred yards long. Walking the piles of slash was like walking on large log jams, but it was an improvement over swimming through the alder thickets. I spent the next half hour picking huckleberries, eating lunch, and figuring the next step to get above the logged area to reach the alpine.

I started up the dry creekbed toward the old growth forest, delayed only by ripe salmon berries, which were at their peak flavor. Upon reaching a dry waterfall too steep for climbing, I had to detour through the forest. The hiking was better back on the creekbed. It was solid granite with few cobbles and log jambs—about ten feet wide, and it was easier hiking than most trails. It was like walking up a series of steps, and there was just enough water trickling down for drinking. Also there were several small falls that I photographed. I could have taken a million pictures walking up this creek. It reminded me of Harbor Steps in Seattle.

An hour and a half of climbing up the creek, including three detours, brought me to the alpine at tree line. By now it was one o'clock, the time I had picked for returning. The peaks above called me, so what else could I do but proceed onward and upward? The best hiking was ahead, traversing large granite and heather terraces. The views to the west were outstanding. After an hour of hiking the granite and heather terraces, I reached the north peak. It was now two o'clock—an hour past my turn around time. The south peak which is a large knob with cliffs on three sides did not appear to be far away. The knob is the highest peak on the mountain. What was another half an hour?

A traverse across a snowfield and I was there. The backside of the knob was terraced and provided an easy scramble to the top. More pictures and it was time to start down the mountain. It was 2:30 P.M. It had taken eight hours from dingy to mountain top. I had to make better time going down to reach the dingy before dark. I proceeded down the granite terraces, snowfields, the almost dry creek, across the slash piles, through the alder thickets, down the logging road, and reached the dingy at eight o'clock. My feet were sore after thirteen and a half hours of hiking.

This hike would be better as an overnight. There are several other peaks and promontories to explore for more views if a person had more time on the mountain.

Journal Entry #50
A Surreal Pictograph Experience
August 4, 2006
Homfray Channel, Desolation Sound

I don't know if it is the genes from my great-great-grandmother that married an Indian translator, or what, but we discovered a pictograph by accident that was totally legible to me. We were starting down Homfray Channel from Atwood Bay and Captain Bob wanted a photograph of the mountain he had climbed the day before. While jockeying for the perfect photo-op, I noticed a red splotch on some rocks. Investigating, we found a small pictograph and as soon as we got close, I knew what it meant! There was no doubt in my mind. It was as if someone told me. I put the engine on idle, then reversed to back up the Shadowfax to the spot that I felt was right.

I told Captain Bob to lower a buzz-bomb down, and as soon as he did, he caught a small rockfish on his first fishing attempt. He started to put the pole away, but I asked him to try again. This time he pulled up an eight pound Yellow-Eye (Red Snapper). I now know what a gambler feels like when he knows a number is going to "come up" and places all of his money on that particular number. At least we were not using money to gamble—just buzz-bombs for fishing.

Journal Entry #51
The Cadborosaurus Willsi of Homfray Channel
August 6, 2006
Lund, Desolation Sound

The oral history of First Nations Peoples of this area describe various sea monsters called by tongue twisting names such as Hiaschuckoluk, T'chain-ko, Sisuitl, Say-Noth-Kai, Na-Ha-Tik, Chunacklas, and Hiyitl'iik—"he who moves by wriggling side to side" in the fjords and inlets of British Columbia. In the 1930's supposed sightings of this sea-going dinosaur or reptile were so horrifying that the creature was given the name of "Sea Hag" by non-native locals. Later sightings near Victoria's Cadboro Bay caused the creature to be christened "Cadborosaurus" (nickname "Caddy"), which was lengthened to Cadborosaurus willsi when presented to the Royal Zoological Society. Much of this information comes from a book *Cadborosaurus: Survivor from the Deep* by Paul H. Leblond and Edward L. Bousfield.

This creature resembles the sea serpents in ancient lore—it has a long neck, lots of sharp teeth, camel like head, fins, flippers, long, snake-like body and of course, it is big. The smaller females "only" measure sixty feet long and have been seen coming into shallow waters where they give birth. Such creatures have allegedly been sighted in the Victoria, BC area as well as in Desolation Sound, with sightings in Homfray Channel where my fishing lure was stolen.

Sounds a lot like the Loch Ness monster, doesn't it?

Like Nessie, this creature has been seen by many people, including groups of thirty or more who saw the apparition frolicking in Cadboro Bay. I did wonder why at least one person in the group didn't have a camera. The only physical traces of this dinosaur are the partially digested remains allegedly found in a sperm whale's tummy in 1937, and the resulting two blurry photographs.

One baby reportedly was found on our own John's Island in the San Juan Islands in 1991. It was stranded on the beach there and returned to the sea by a compassionate islander. (She didn't have a camera, either.) The lady was known to be a little odd by the local islanders, so her Caddy "sighting" might be considered suspicious.

Maybe a Cadborosaurus was what sampled my fake octopus in Atwood Bay, either that or a halibut or a six-gill shark. Perhaps the pictograph in Homfray Channel supposedly depicting a sea serpent being ridden by a brave (or totally foolhardy) person is the first written/pictorial record of this creature.

A number of websites provided intriguing information, factual or not: www.cryptomundo.com, www.oraclevision.ca, www.bcscc.ca, www.cryptozoology.freeservers.com and http://www.s8int.com/dino23.html. These sites also mentioned scientific texts that support the existence of Cadborosaurus. The information might be suspect, but the names of the articles, books, and headlines are impressive: *Canadian Sea Serpent Officially Recognized by Science.*

Cadborosaurus willsi; New Genus, New species source: *The Hieronimus & Co. Newlsletter,* Vol. 1, No. 7. An article in *Amphipacifica Journal of Systematic Biology* by Drs. Paul H. LeBlond and Edward L. Bousfield also reviews "the large aquatic reptile known as 'Caddy' from the Pacific coast of North America." Describing its "distinctive head, long neck, and trunk region that often appear formed into a number of vertical humps or loops, its swimming speed is astonishing to those who try to approach it, invariably unsuccessfully."

Caddy would not be the first animal that was formerly thought extinct to be officially recognized as alive and well in the 20th century. Through the efforts of cryptozoologists (people who study lost or hidden animals) our planet has proved to still contain surprises, especially in the deep seas and inaccessible jungles. For example, in 1938 somebody discovered a living Coelacanth, a lobed armored fish, which populated the seas 64 million years ago and was thought to be extinct. Since then, more than a dozen Coelacanths have been caught or beached. In 1976 somebody caught an unknown kind of shark off the island of Oahu in the Hawaiian Islands. The 14.5 foot shark was later named Megamouth.

Sea Serpents have been reported and documented for centuries in the seas and lakes all around the globe and cryptozoologists have used all of 20th century's best technology to try to officially document their continued existence. There is Scotland's Loch Ness Monster, Chessie of the Chesapeake Bay area of Virginia, Ogopogo of Canada's Lake Okanogan, and Champ of upstate New York's Lake Champlain.

As if to underscore the worldwide area the Cadborosaurus is found in, the eastern twin located a carved wooden likeness of "Caddy" obtained from the Amazon River area in South America by the Cousteau Society. The carving is housed at the society's office in Virginia. The pictures depict a creature uncannily resembling the creature that Dr. Bousfield and Dr. Leblond describe—especially since one special characteristic of the sea serpent is that its head is camel shaped.

Journal Entry #52
Three Hundred Fifty Year Old Portrait
August 8, 2006
Homfray Channel, Desolation Sound

Using vague descriptions mentioned in the book *High Slack* by Judith Williams, we managed to locate some pictographs that were very old. One figure is supposedly Quodham, probably a chieftain, complete with headdress. There are schools of fish, a strange horned, finned long creature (Cadborosaurus?), a canoe with two paddlers and possibly salmon weirs—all created in red salmon paste pigment. All were supposedly created over 350 years ago, according to the book. The figures are very red and very clear for such aged images.

Our grandson, Tor, was entranced with the designs and grabbed a video camera to commemorate our find. Then he tried fishing to see if the fish were still present after 350 years, but no such luck.

We are seeing a similarity between pictograph sites. They were created above the high water mark on a white rocky cliff. Some were under some form of overhang and had water access. My guess is that the overhang protected the drying salmon egg paste from the elements until it cured. The salmon eggs would have been readily available in the fall at the start of the rainy season, so perhaps that is when these images were created.

There may have been other designs created on the surrounding shoreline, but without some form of rocky overhang protecting the pigments they would have faded to invisibility or been washed away by the rain.

One fish pictograph perfectly legible when dry became almost invisible in the rain when the rocks darkened with dampness. So maybe more pictures are just in hiding, waiting for the perfect time to reappear and once again tell the tales of the First Nations from long ago.

Journal Entry #53
The LACC Burgee
August 16, 2006
Desolation Sound to Meydenbauer Bay, Bellevue

One of the last purchases made for the Shadowfax before the start of our travels north was a *Latitudes and Attitudes* (a sailing magazine) membership. We were issued a plastic card with our proud membership number, information on club benefits, and a beautiful LACC burgee, which was immediately hung from our halyards to fly aloft during our entire voyage. The sea serpent decorating the burgee even resembled, appropriately enough, our own Pacific Northwest Cadborosaurus!

As we traveled the Inside Passage north to Alaska from Seattle and back we had not a single sighting of a fellow LACC burgee. Not even in August in Desolation Sound where Squirrel Cove boasted over a hundred and thirty boats anchored in its snug harbor one summer evening. In fact all the harbors were so crowded with vacationers it was hard to find room to anchor—very different from the Desolation Sound of May and June. We saw many sailing vessels, but none flying LACC burgees. The Shadowfax flew a lonesome flag indeed.

We slowly worked our way in a southerly direction, sailing and fishing, whenever possible, down Malispina Strait, across the Straits of Georgia to finally find moorage in Nanaimo Harbor. We were nearing the end of our adventure and this is where we planned to leave the Shadowfax with Captain Bob for him to do the final sprint to Seattle, sailing solo. Our grandson needed to be escorted back across the border and the two of us had planned to fly out on a seaplane to Seattle and home. This was accomplished with only one hitch.

After cheerfully waving to the departing Shadowfax, we realized we had mistakenly identified the seaplane pickup site. We had to hike three miles (along with backpacks and gear) in sixty minutes in the hot sun to catch the plane. We did it!

Captain Bob made the final portion of the trip alone with an exhilarating sail across the Straits of Juan De Fuca with a co-operating Shadowfax. A rendezvous was planned at Shilshole Bay Marina in Seattle to pick up a crew member for the trip through the locks and the boat's final destination of Meydenbauer Bay. As the Shadowfax docked in Shilshole for the pickup, the imposing Department of Homeland Security boat showed up, complete with strapping muscular young men adorned with black bulletproof vests, big boots, uniforms, and guns.

They were extremely intimidating as were their tattoos and haircuts. We tried to look innocent and carefully refrained from jokes, conversation, or even eye contact and were thankfully ignored. The young guards were more interested in purchasing goodies from the snack bar, such as cookies, candy, pop, and items that looked like they might once have been fresh warm hamburgers than they were in boarding the Shadowfax. As we left Shilshole, we had our first and only sighting of a fellow LACC burgee, appropriately enough flying from the halyards of a sailing vessel named "Ghost" moored at the docks. Its burgee wasn't faded or shredded like the burgee the Shadowfax now flew, so perhaps it hadn't flown up the Inside Passage and back yet.

To order additional copies of this title call:
1-877-421-READ (7323)
or please visit our Web site at
www.annotationbooks.com

If you enjoyed this quality custom-published book,
drop by our Web site for more books and information.

www.winepressgroup.com
"Your partner in custom publishing."

LaVergne, TN USA
30 November 2009
165331LV00002B